WILDERNESS NAVIGATION

Finding Your Way Using Map, Compass, Altimeter & GPS

FOURTH EDITION

Bob Burns & Mike Burns

MOUNTAINEERS
BOOKS

To the memories of the teachers, mentors, and lifelong friends who have gone before us, including Clinton Kelley, Richard Kaylor, Erhard Wichert, Alex Lowe, Norm Wynn, Jim Giblin, and Scott Fischer. Without their friendship, knowledge, and leadership, some of us would be lost in the wilderness of life.

MOUNTAINEERS BOOKS is dedicated to the exploration, preservation, and enjoyment of outdoor and wilderness areas.

1001 SW Klickitat Way, Suite 201, Seattle, WA 98134
800-553-4453, www.mountaineersbooks.org

Printed in China
First edition, 1999. Second edition, 2004. Third edition, 2015. Fourth edition, 2025.

Design and layout: Kate Basart, unionpageworks.com
Original illustrations: Jennifer Shontz, Red Shoe Design;
updated and adapted for the fourth edition: Chloé Dorgan
Maps on pages 56 and 57 by Ellis Failor-Rich; pages 58 and 167 by Lohnes + Wright
Front cover photograph: Map and compass (Silas Crews)
Back cover photograph: *Woman checking altimeter* (Izf/Shutterstock)
Frontispiece: *Trekking toward the high peaks of the Wind River Range, Wyoming* (Alex Moliski)

Library of Congress Cataloging-in-Publication data is on file for this title at
https://lccn.loc.gov/2024948093

Mountaineers Books titles may be purchased for corporate, educational, or other promotional sales, and our authors are available for a wide range of events. For information on special discounts or booking an author, contact our customer service at 800-553-4453 or mbooks@mountaineersbooks.org.

Printed on FSC®-certified materials

ISBN (paperback): 978-1-68051-721-7
ISBN (ebook): 978-1-68051-722-4

An independent nonprofit publisher since 1960

WILDERNESS
NAVIGATION

Contents

Preface

The origins of this book are lost among the rough notes of The Mountaineers' first climbing course, held in 1935. They were eventually published in 1960 as *Mountaineering: The Freedom of the Hills*, a comprehensive mountain climbing book that covers the necessary equipment, navigation and wilderness travel skills, and technical aspects of climbing on rock,

snow, glaciers, and expeditions. *Freedom*, as it is commonly called, has been revised nine times since its initial publication, and we have authored or coauthored its navigation chapter in six of those revisions.

In addition to writing about navigation, we have hiked, scrambled, snowshoed, and climbed extensively, as well as taught navigation skills in courses sponsored by The Mountaineers. In some of the nonclimbing classes, we were often asked to recommend a book covering the material

presented in our courses. Prior to 1999, the only book using the same methods and covering the same material was *Freedom*. Some skiers, snowshoers, and hikers balked at buying a book that covered technical rock and ice climbing in detail just to obtain information on backcountry navigation. It was out of this need that the idea for *Wilderness Navigation* emerged. First published in 1999, it was revised in 2004 and again in 2015. This fourth edition brings it further up to date on the newest technology and trends in wilderness navigation.

The Mountaineers have taught these methods of using maps and compasses since the 1990s. Through this approach, orienting the map, adding or subtracting declination, and drawing declination lines on maps are not necessary. Instead, you will learn how to use baseplate compasses with adjustable declination and how to make nonadjustable baseplate compasses work the same way, which has proven to be an easy and dependable method of dealing with declination.

This edition incorporates significant recent changes in the types and availability of topographical maps, changes in magnetic declination, and changes to be consistent with the tenth edition of *Mountaineering: The Freedom of the Hills*, as well as the development of satellite-based navigational products. We have also updated this edition in response to questions and suggestions from readers, added full-color map examples scanned from original US Geological Survey files, and included new illustrations and photographs.

We invite any reader with questions, comments, or suggestions for improvement to contact Mountaineers Books.

Introduction

Where am I? How far is it to my destination? Will I be able to find my way back? This book shows how to use orientation and navigation to answer these most frequently asked questions. The tools and techniques are simple and straightforward—but exacting. Study them carefully to help make your wilderness adventures successful and to keep you safe and within the ranks of surviving navigators. Before you immerse yourself in this book, remember that navigation is easy and fun. (So much fun, in fact, that some people engage in the sport of orienteering, in which participants compete with others using a map and compass to get to various destinations on a structured course.) First, a few definitions:

Wilderness, as used in this book, is considered to be any area away from human-made features such as roads, structures, electricity, cell phone antennas, and other modern conveniences, where travelers are dependent on their own abilities and resources for travel and survival.

Orientation is the science of determining your exact position on Earth.

Navigation is the science of determining the location of your objective and keeping yourself on the correct path from your starting point toward this destination and back.

Routefinding is the art of selecting and following the best path appropriate for the abilities and equipment of the party.

The route through this book is divided into two parts. The first, consisting of chapters 1 through 6, contains information on maps, compasses, orientation, navigation, altimeters, satellite-based navigation and communication devices, how to avoid getting lost, and what to do if you *do* get lost. These chapters contain the basic essentials of wilderness navigation for all wilderness travelers, including those who never intend to leave a well-maintained trail. A thorough understanding of these chapters is essential for all wilderness travelers.

Chapters 7 and 8 provide more advanced information on the latitude/longitude and Universal Transverse Mercator (UTM) coordinate systems; distance measurement and pace; the use of clinometers; and more detailed information on maps, geomagnetism, global travel, and wilderness routefinding. We recommend a careful reading of these chapters for anyone who intends to leave the trail and venture cross-country in search of hidden fishing lakes, challenging mountain peaks, interesting cross-country ski routes, and other destinations beyond the well-maintained trail, or for foreign travel to distant lands. These chapters are also important for those who choose to use the Global Positioning System (GPS).

Whichever route you choose, we highly recommend reading chapter 8, Wilderness Routefinding. Although some of it may not apply to those who never intend to leave a well-worn trail, there is much in the last chapter that applies to all wilderness navigators.

If you do not own a compass, we suggest that you read chapters 1 and 2 before buying one.

We also highly recommend that you complete the Skills Checks at the end of every chapter as you navigate through this book. Answers are given in the appendix.

This book will *not* make you an expert in wilderness navigation; only practice and experience will do that. But it can give you a basic foundation in the skills necessary for safe and enjoyable wilderness travel.

A NOTE ABOUT SAFETY

Safety is an important concern in all outdoor activities. No guidebook can alert you to every hazard or anticipate the limitations of every reader. Therefore, the descriptions of techniques and procedures in this book are intended to provide general information. This is not a complete text on wilderness travel. Nothing substitutes for formal instruction, routine practice, and plenty of experience. When you engage in any of the activities described in this book, you assume responsibility for your own safety. Under normal conditions, excursions into the backcountry require the usual attention to traffic, road and trail conditions, local regulations, weather, terrain, the capabilities of your party, and other factors. Keeping informed on current conditions and exercising common sense are the keys to a safe, enjoyable outing.

—**Mountaineers Books**

CHAPTER 1

MAP BASICS

CHAPTER OBJECTIVES

- Learn basic map terminology.
- Understand how to read topographic maps, including declination, reference (meridian) lines, colors, contour lines, datum, and slope direction.
- Identify the limitations of maps.
- Learn the best ways to customize and carry maps for wilderness adventures.
- Be able to get maps and create your own.

A map is a symbolic picture of a place. It conveys a phenomenal amount of information in a form that is easy to understand and easy to carry. No one should venture into the wilderness without a map or chart of the area, nor without the skills required to interpret and thoroughly understand it. Note that the subtitle of this book is *Finding Your Way Using Map, Compass, Altimeter & GPS*; the order of these words was chosen deliberately to list these four items in order from highest priority: first, a map, then a compass, altimeter, and GPS.

You can find a lot of useful information on a map. For water activities, navigational charts provide the same level of information as topographic maps do on land, but with particular attention to navigational hazards. For wilderness land travel, the most important items are topographic features, vegetation, and elevation information, which are discussed in this chapter. (See chapter 7 for more in-depth information, such as the use of various coordinate systems, distance and slope measurement, and survey information.) Note the publication date of the map, because roads, trails, and other features may have changed since the map was printed.

Understanding Map Types and Terms

The **scale** of a map is a ratio between measurements on the map and measurements in the real world. A common way to state the scale is to compare a map measurement with a ground measurement (e.g., 1 inch on a particular map equals 1 mile in the field) or to give a specific mathematical ratio (e.g., 1:24,000 is the scale most commonly used in the United States, where any one unit of measure on the map equals 24,000 units of the same measure on Earth).

Several different types of maps are available. **Relief maps** attempt to show terrain in three dimensions by using various shades of green, gray, and brown; terrain sketching; and raised surfaces. They help you visualize the ups and downs of the landscape and have some value in trip planning. Relief maps are often displayed at visitor centers in national parks and recreation areas.

Land management and recreation maps—published by the US Forest Service, the National Park Service, other government agencies, National Geographic, and timber companies—are frequently updated and are very useful for determining the current conditions and locations of roads, trails, ranger stations, and other human-made structures. They usually show only the horizontal relationship of natural features, without contour lines indicating the shape of the land. These maps are often helpful for trip planning.

Sketch maps tend to be crudely drawn but often make up in specialized route detail what they lack in draftsmanship. Such drawings can be effective supplements to other map and guidebook information.

Guidebook maps vary greatly in quality. Some are merely sketches, while others are accurate modifications of topographic maps. They often contain useful details on roads, trails, and wilderness routes.

Topographic maps are the best of all for wilderness travelers. They depict topography, the shape of Earth's surface, by showing **contour lines** that represent constant elevations above and below sea level. These maps, essential to off-trail travel, are produced in most countries. They should be carried on all wilderness excursions, along with any of the other above-mentioned maps. Some are produced by government agencies, such as the US Geological Survey (USGS), whereas others are printed by private companies. Some private companies produce maps based on

USGS maps and update them with recent trail and road details, sometimes combining sections of different USGS maps into a single map. One example is Green Trails Maps, which makes maps for mountain areas in the Pacific Northwest as well as selected portions of the southwestern United States. These maps are useful supplements to standard topographic maps and are particularly helpful for trail hiking. As an example of topographic maps, we will look in detail at USGS maps.

USGS Topographic Maps

The USGS map most commonly used by wilderness travelers in the United States outside of Alaska covers an area of 7.5 minutes (i.e., ⅛ degree) of latitude by 7.5 minutes of longitude. These maps are known as the **7.5-minute series**. An older type of USGS map covers an area of 15 minutes (i.e., ¼ degree) of latitude by 15 minutes of longitude. These maps are part of what is called the **15-minute series**. Four 7.5-minute maps are needed to cover the same area as one 15-minute map. The 7.5-minute maps depict topographic features much more clearly than the 15-minute maps do.

The 7.5-minute map is the standard for the contiguous United States and Hawaii and is the most commonly used type for wilderness travelers in the United States outside of Alaska:

- The scale is 1:24,000, or roughly 2.5 inches to the mile, or approximately 4 centimeters (cm) to the kilometer (km).
- Each map covers an area of approximately 6 miles by 9 miles (10 kilometers by 14 kilometers), and the UTM squares are 1 kilometer on a side.

> **Tip:** In Canada, Mexico, and most of the rest of the world where the metric system is used, the most commonly used comparable scale is 1:50,000. Scales of 1:25,000 and others are occasionally used as well.

The 15-minute map is the standard for Alaska, due to its size:

- The scale is 1:63,360, or exactly 1 inch to 1 mile, or 1.6 centimeters to 1 kilometer. The north–south extent of each Alaska map is 15 minutes, but the east–west extent is greater than 15 minutes, because the lines of longitude converge toward the North Pole.

- Each map covers an area of about 12 to 16 miles (19 to 26 kilometers) east–west and 18 miles (29 kilometers) north–south.

Topographic Map Features

The USGS currently distributes two types of topographic maps for every area in the United States: "Historical" maps produced predominantly in the twentieth century and "US Topo" maps produced mostly in the twenty-first century. Both types are useful to wilderness travelers. The differences between these two map types will be explained later in this chapter; what follows here is a description of map characteristics common to both.

Each USGS map is referred to as a **quadrangle** (or "quad") and covers an area bounded on the north and south by latitude lines that differ by an amount equal to the map series (7.5 minutes or 15 minutes) and on the east and west by longitude lines that differ by the same amount, except for Alaska.

To read a topographic map, you'll need to be familiar with these key map features: colors, contour lines, declination, datum and meridian lines, and slope direction.

COLORS

Colors on a USGS topographic map have specific meanings:

Red: Major roads and survey information.

Blue: Rivers, lakes, springs, waterfalls, marshes, glaciers, and permanent snowfields.

Black or gray: Minor roads, trails, railroads, structures, benchmarks, UTM coordinates, and other human-related features.

Green: Solid green indicates a forest. A lack of green does not mean that an area is devoid of vegetation but rather that any growth is too small or scattered to show on the map. Contour lines and elevations of index contours are brown. Scattered green markings in flat areas indicate wetlands.

White with blue contour lines: Used on historical USGS maps, this indicates a glacier or permanent snowfield. Contour lines are in solid blue, with their edges indicated by dashed blue lines. Elevations are shown in blue. Rope up for all glacier travel!

White with blue speckles: Used on US Topo maps, this indicates glaciers and permanent snowfields. Elevations and contour lines are shown in brown.

White with brown contour lines: Any area without substantial forest, such as a high alpine area, a clear-cut, a rockslide, an avalanche gully, or a meadow. Study the map for other clues.

Purple: Partial revision of an existing map.

Always be aware of the temporal nature of map features, since logging, glacial expansion or recession, volcanic activity, and other changes might have occurred since the map was last updated.

CONTOUR LINES

The heart of a topographic map is its overlay of contour lines, each line indicating a constant elevation as it follows the shape of the landscape. A map's **contour interval** is the difference in elevation between any two adjacent contour lines. The contour interval is clearly printed at the bottom of the map. Every fifth contour line, called an **index contour**, is printed darker than the other lines and is labeled with the elevation.

One of the most important bits of information a topographic map reveals is whether you will be traveling uphill or downhill. If the route crosses lines of increasingly higher elevation, you will be going uphill. If it crosses lines of decreasing elevation, the route is downhill. Level or sidehill travel is indicated by a route that crosses no lines, remaining within a single contour interval.

Topographic maps also show cliffs, passes, summits, and other features (fig. 1-1). Main features depicted by contour lines include the following:

Flat or nearly flat areas: No lines at all over a certain area (no elevation differences of more than the contour interval, such as 40 feet in these examples). The area in figure 1-1a also has a lake and a surrounding wetland area.

Gentle slopes: Widely spaced contour lines. The example in figure 1-1b is gentle enough for the roads shown.

Steep slopes: Closely spaced contour lines. The one shown in figure 1-1c is too steep for a road.

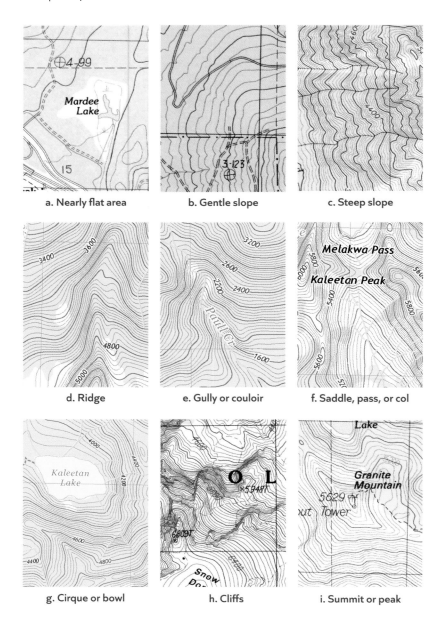

Fig. 1-1. *Basic topographic features*

Ridges or spurs: Contour lines in a pattern of Us for gentle, rounded ridges; Vs for sharp ridges (fig. 1-1d). The Us and Vs point downhill, in the direction of lower elevation.

Gullies, couloirs, valleys, and ravines: Contour lines in a pattern of Us for gentle, rounded valleys or gullies; Vs for sharp valleys and gullies (fig. 1-1e). The Us and Vs point uphill, in the direction of higher elevation. Many rivers and creeks flow through stream gullies, like Paull Creek in the example shown.

Saddles, passes, or cols: An hourglass shape (with higher contour lines on two opposite sides), indicating a low point on a ridge (fig. 1-1f). These are often useful for wilderness travel, frequently providing travelers with the path of lowest elevation and least effort to cross a mountain ridge.

Cirques or bowls: Patterns of contour lines forming at least a semicircle, rising from a low spot in the center to form a natural amphitheater at the head of a valley. Some contain lakes (fig. 1-1g).

Cliffs: Contour lines extremely close together or even touching. The example shown (fig. 1-1h) is near the rocky summit of Washington State's Mount Olympus, which is so steep that snow cannot accumulate, as it does on the nearby glaciers.

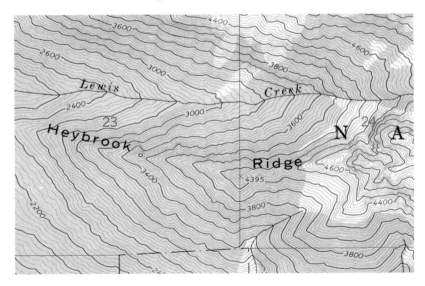

Fig. 1-2. *Ridge and gully compared*

Summits or peaks: A concentric pattern of contour lines, with the summit being the innermost and highest ring (fig. 1-1i). Peaks are also often indicated by Xs, elevations, benchmarks (BMs), or triangle symbols.

Most of these contour line patterns are easy to interpret and sufficiently unique so that there is little chance for misinterpreting them. Ridges and gullies are an exception. For these features, the contour line patterns look very similar. For example, figure 1-2 shows topographic map depictions of both a ridge and a gully in close proximity, so that you can easily compare them. Note that the contour line patterns for Heybrook Ridge all point in the direction of lower elevation, while those for nearby Lewis Creek gully all point in the direction of higher elevation. If you ever forget whether uphill-pointing or downhill-pointing contour lines indicate ridges or gullies, just look at the contour lines around a thin blue line on a map indicating a stream, keeping in mind that *streams usually flow down gullies*, and never on ridges.

Before you venture into the wilderness, we suggest that you carefully study figures 1-3 through 1-6 on the next few pages to gain an appreciation of how various features shown in photographs appear on topographic maps.

> **Tip:** As you travel in the wilderness, frequently observe the terrain and associate its appearance with its depiction on your map. Note all the topographic features—such as ridges, gullies, streams, and summits—as you pass them. This helps you maintain a close estimate of where you are and helps you become an expert map reader.

DECLINATION INFORMATION

The margins of USGS maps contain the date of publication and revision, contour intervals, map scales, and the area's **magnetic declination** at the time the map was last updated. **Declination** is the difference between true north and magnetic north. Declination is extremely important and will be discussed in more detail in chapters 2 and 7. Depending on the type of map and publication date, declination is labeled differently:

Fig. 1-3. Photograph of a mountainous area and its depiction on a corresponding topographic map: **A,** photo taken from here, in direction shown; **B,** gentle slope; **C,** moderate slope; **D,** trail along hillside; **E,** ridge crest; **F,** saddle along ridge crest; **G,** minor summit on ridge; **H,** skyline ridge

Fig. 1-4. *Photograph of mountain peaks and their depiction on a corresponding topographic map:* **A,** *photograph taken from this location, in direction shown;* **B,** *saddle or col;* **C,** *twin summits;* **D,** *cliff;* **E,** *moderate slope;* **F,** *steep slope;* **G,** *ridges*

Fig. 1-5. *Photograph of a mountainous area and its depiction on a topographic map, illustrating various topographic features:* **A,** *ridge crest;* **B,** *secondary summit;* **C,** *saddle (pass);* **D,** *major gully descending from saddle;* **E,** *ridge crest;* **F,** *steep slope;* **G,** *primary summit;* **H,** *very steep slope;* **I,** *nearly level area;* **J,** *broad forested ridge;* **K,** *direction of photograph*

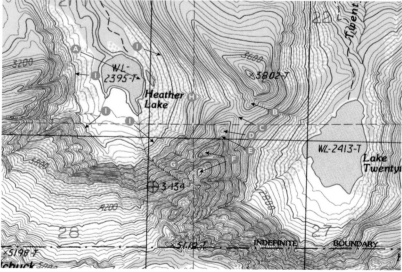

Fig. 1-6. *Photograph of a mountain cirque and its depiction on a topographic map:* **A,** *photograph taken from here, in direction shown;* **B,** *moderately steep (30°) ridge;* **C,** *low point on ridge (saddle; note the hourglass-shaped pattern of contour lines on the map);* **D,** *small forested knoll;* **E,** *steep (60°) ridge;* **F,** *pinnacles;* **G,** *very steep cliffs below pinnacles;* **H,** *broad gully between saddle and lake;* **I,** *contour line nearly encircling lake, a classic characteristic of a cirque*

- Historical USGS maps printed before 1988, as well as the newer US Topo maps printed in the twenty-first century, usually have a declination diagram printed at the bottom of the map (fig. 1-7A). The angle difference between these two directions is the magnetic declination for that area at the time the map was last updated.
- Provisional historical USGS maps printed mostly in the late 1980s and early 1990s (fig. 1-7B) have a statement in their lower-left corner, such as "1989 MAGNETIC NORTH DECLINATION 19°30' EAST" near a north arrow pointing to the top of the map.

DATUM AND MERIDIAN (NORTH–SOUTH) LINES

A map's **datum** is a reference point on which to base your position. In the United States, the North American Datum of 1927 (NAD 27) was used as this reference for most of the twentieth century. Maps produced in the twenty-first century, including the US Topo series, use the World Geodetic System of 1984 (WGS 84). In the United States, this is equivalent to NAD 83. WGS84 is also used by the Global Positioning System (GPS). The datum is printed in the lower-left corner of the map (see figs. 1-7A and B). The importance of the datum will be described in chapter 5.

Meridian (north–south) lines run north–south on maps; they are very important for using the map with a compass, as will be explained in chapter 2. Most newer maps (published after 1988) have a grid of UTM lines printed on the map (fig. 1-7B), and these can be used as north–south reference lines or meridian lines. This grid is usually slightly offset from true north, because the map is attempting to represent our spherical planet on a flat surface, therefore introducing a slight error. The amount of this offset is given in the lower-left corner of the map, such as by a number next to GN (grid north) on a declination diagram (1°10' GN in fig. 1-7A), or with a statement such as "UTM GRID DECLINATION 1°09' EAST" (in fig. 1-7B). Vertical UTM lines may also be used as a north–south reference, but only if the grid offset is less than 2 degrees. If the UTM grid offset is more than 2 degrees, if the UTM grid lines are too faint, or if there are no UTM lines (as in fig. 1-7A), you can draw in your own north–south lines by placing the long side of a straightedge (such as a meter stick or a yard-stick) along the left margin of the map and drawing a line along the other

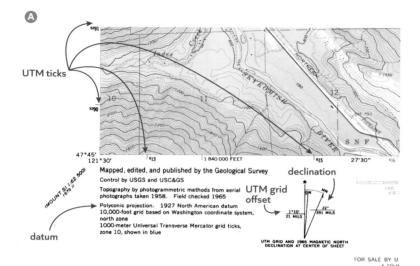

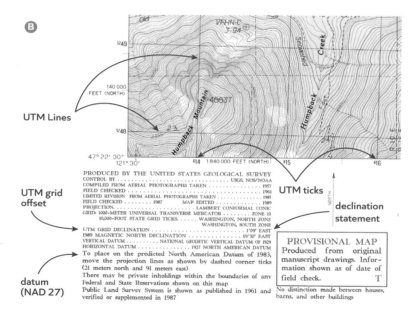

Fig. 1-7. *Declination and UTM information:* **A,** *on most USGS maps other than provisional;* **B,** *on provisional USGS maps*

side of the straightedge. Then move the straightedge over to the line you just drew and draw another line, and repeat. This way, you will have a set of north–south lines that are truly north–south. This will help you achieve accuracy in measuring and plotting bearings on the map using your compass, as will be explained in chapter 2.

TWO TYPES OF USGS TOPOGRAPHICAL MAPS

Two main types of topographical maps are presently available for the United States from the USGS.

The entire United States was mapped in the twentieth century. In the late 1980s and early 1990s, many of these original topographic maps were updated using the original topographical data with changes due to

Table 1-1. COMPARISON OF USGS HISTORICAL AND US TOPO MAPS		
Map characteristics	**Historical maps**	**US Topo maps**
Hiking trails	Most trails shown.	Some trails not shown. USGS working on updating Topo maps.
Glaciers and snowfields*	Elevations of index contours are in blue; edges are dashed blue lines. Glacier extent may not be up to date.	Contour lines and index contour elevations are in brown; glaciers have blue speckles. Edges of glaciers are not shown. Glacier extent is more accurate.
Mountain summit names and elevations	Names and elevations of most mountains shown.	Most names shown; most elevations are not shown. Approximate elevations can be found by contour lines.
Data shown on map or can be added to it	Contain topographic data only (roads, trails, lakes, etc.).	In addition to topographic data, contain many different "layers," such as hydrographic; some such information is not important for hikers.
Human-made features and recent natural events (roads, structures, etc.)	May be years out of date; may not show recent logging.	Up to date to within a few years for most human-caused activity.

*Many glaciers and snowfields are disappearing or receding as of this writing.

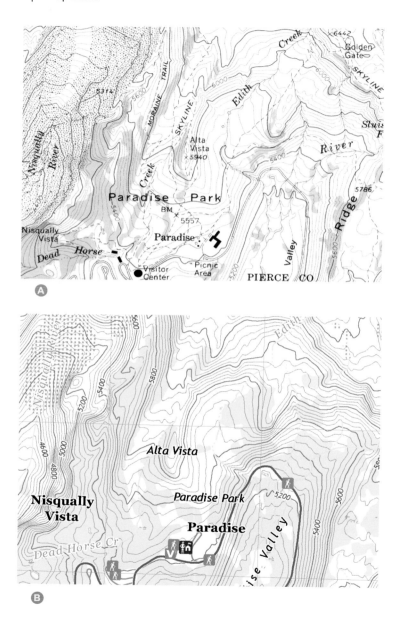

Fig. 1-8. *USGS Mount Rainier East, Paradise area:* **A,** *1971 historical map;* **B,** *2020 US Topo map*

logging, road construction, the addition of human-made structures, and other causes. These updated maps are referred to as "provisional" maps. Both the original twentieth-century maps and the updated provisional maps are now referred to as "historical" and are still available from the USGS and other map dealers. These maps are still frequently used by many wilderness travelers today.

In the early twenty-first century, a new type of topographic map technology was developed, based on satellite data and modern digital technology. These are referred to as US Topo maps; they cover the same areas and have the same names as the historical maps but have publication dates from the year 2000 onward. Both types of maps have advantages and disadvantages, as well as some noticeable visual differences. Table 1-1 summarizes the characteristics of both the historical and the US Topo maps, so you can decide which map type to purchase for your particular activity. Of special interest to most foot travelers is the depiction of trails. Many trails depicted on the historical maps are not yet shown on some US Topo maps, though the USGS says that the historical trails will eventually be added as time and resources allow. We recommend that you carefully examine the products available for both types of maps at store.usgs.gov to determine which is best for you. In particular, if you plan on hiking a certain trail, ensure that it is shown on the map before you purchase it.

Examples of some of these differences are shown in figures 1-8 and 1-9. Figure 1-8A shows the Paradise area on Mount Rainier on the 1971 historical map, while figure 1-8B shows the same area on a 2020 US Topo map. By comparing the historical and Topo maps, you can see where human-made features, such as the location of the visitor center, have been added, moved, or removed. Many of the hiking trails shown in the 1971 map are not yet shown in the 2020 US Topo map. Some glaciers and snowfields shown on the historical map from 1971 are not shown on the 2020 map since they have receded or disappeared due to melting.

Figure 1-9 shows the Camp Schurman area of Mount Rainier, near its 9500-foot level. Figure 1-9A is from the 1971 historical map, while figure 1-9B is from the 2020 US Topo map. Of particular interest is the depiction of glaciers. In the historical map, the glacier's contour lines and

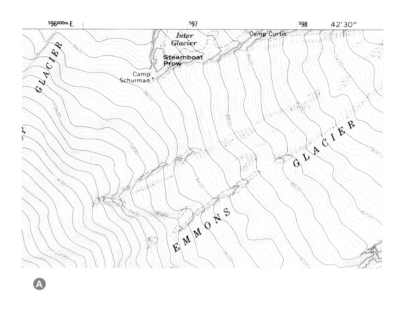

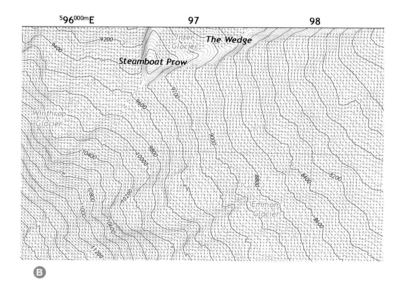

Fig. 1-9. *USGS Mount Rainier East, Camp Schurman area:* **A,** *1971 historical map;* **B,** *2020 US Topo map*

index contour elevations are in blue, while the edges are shown by dashed blue lines. The US Topo map shows the glacier with blue speckles on a white background, and its contour lines and index contour elevations are in brown. The edges of the glacier are not shown but can be inferred by noting where the blue speckles end.

Because historical and US Topo maps both have unique benefits, you can combine information from both into one map containing the features you need. For example, if the historical map of an area shows an important feature such as a trail, but the US Topo map does not show the trail, or if it shows that a new road has been built or an old road has been extended or closed, you can buy the historical map and copy the newly updated information from the USGS website onto it. You can also buy the updated US Topo map and copy the trail location from the historical map onto it.

DIRECTION OF THE SLOPE

Traveling along a contour line means traveling on a roughly level route. Conversely, traveling in the direction perpendicular (at a right angle) to a

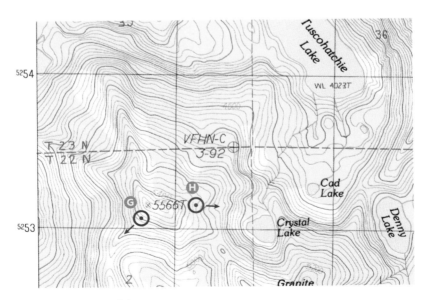

Fig. 1-10. *Direction of slope*

contour line means traveling directly uphill or downhill, sometimes called the **fall line**. The fall line can be a valuable clue as to your position. You can easily find this direction on the map or in the field for any point on sloping terrain. For example, in figure 1-10, point G has a slope that falls off to the southwest. Point H, on the other hand, has a slope falling off roughly to the east. You will be able to express this direction more precisely after you learn how to measure and plot bearings using a compass in chapter 2.

Using the direction of the slope cannot prove that you are at any particular place, but it can often disprove it, and this can help in figuring out exactly where you are (that is, your orientation). In figure 1-10, for example, suppose you have climbed Peak 5566 and have descended a few hundred feet. You wish to find out where you are, and you guess that you are at point G. That means that the slope should be falling off to the southwest. However, when standing on the slope and facing downhill, you can tell from the position of the sun in the sky at that time of the day that you are facing roughly east. This proves that you cannot be at point G. You could very possibly be at point H, since at this point the slope falls off to the east. But there are other places where the slope falls off to the east, so you cannot prove that you are at point H. If you have a fairly close estimate of your altitude, such as that of your last known position or as indicated on an altimeter (see chapter 4), adding the knowledge of direction of slope can often help you to ascertain your position with certainty.

Knowing the Limitations of Maps

There are a couple cautionary thoughts to keep in mind as you study a topographic map. First, *the map will not show all the terrain features* that you actually see on your trip, because there is a limit to what mapmakers can include on the map without reducing it to an unreadable clutter. For example, if a feature is not at least as high as the contour interval, it may not be shown, so a 30-foot cliff may come as a surprise when you are navigating with a map that has a 40-foot contour interval.

Second, *check the publication date of the map*; topographic maps may not be revised very often, and information on forests, roads, and other human-made or naturally occurring features (such as the eruption of a volcano) could be out of date. A forest may have been logged, a glacier may have advanced or receded, or a road may have been extended or closed since the last update. Although topographic maps are essential to wilderness travel, you often need to supplement them with information from rangers, recent visitors to the area, guidebooks, websites, and other maps.

Customizing and Modifying Maps

Sometimes a trip runs through portions of two or more maps. Adjoining maps can be folded at the edges and brought together, or you can create your own customized map by cutting out the nonpertinent areas and splicing the rest together with tape. You can also create maps using a computer and readily available map software such as CalTopo. When customizing maps, be sure to *include plenty of territory* so that you will have a good overview of the entire trip, including the surrounding area (which might be needed for orientation; see chapter 3).

Black-and-white photocopies are good for marking the route, but since they do not show colors, they should be used only as supplements to the real thing. If a durable, high-quality reproduction is needed, then a color photocopy on waterproof paper using a laser (rather than inkjet) printer may be the best approach. Some outdoor recreation stores can produce computer-generated maps covering whatever area you want by combining various sections of USGS quadrangles. Though these customized maps are more expensive than the standard USGS quadrangles, you may appreciate their convenience.

Some wilderness travelers choose to cut off the wide white borders of topographic maps to save weight and bulk. If you do this, be sure to *retain the important information* printed at the bottom and edges of the map, including the scale, contour interval, declination, datum, and UTM zone. This information may be useful to you later. Keep in mind that these blank areas are also good for adding notes, such as updates and corrections.

> **Tip:** When you learn of changes (such as road or trail closures), note them on your map in pencil, along with the date.

Carrying Maps in the Wilderness

One of the most important aspects of carrying a map is to do so in such a way that you can get to it at any time. We suggest that you carry it in your pocket, protected by a plastic map case or a resealable plastic bag.

> **Tip:** Cargo pants or shorts with big pockets are excellent for carrying maps, compasses, and other objects that you need to access quickly. It is a lot easier to make frequent observations if you can get to your map at any time without removing your pack.

MAP FOLDING

When carrying your map, fold it to show the area where you will be traveling, and then place it in your plastic case or resealable bag. This way, it will be protected from the elements, always visible, easy to remove, and compact.

Fold your map so that your entire route for a given leg of the trip is always visible without unfolding the map, if possible. If you keep your map in the pocket of cargo pants or shorts, for example, the folded map should also be slightly smaller than the pocket (approximately 5 by 5 inches or 13 by 13 centimeters). With the finished dimension in mind, fold your map so that your starting point is on one edge of the folded map, and fold up the remaining part of the map so that as much of the route as possible is visible. At the main fold, your route can continue to the other side of the map. It will then be very easy for you to flip your map over to the other side as your day progresses without the need to refold it.

> **Tip:** Try to keep map folds away from key route junctions or other important areas of interest, since folds tend to degrade with time and wear, particularly if the map gets wet.

Another way to keep your map accessible throughout your trip is to fold it to approximately the inner dimensions of your camera case, if you carry one, and carry it inside the case, held on the hip belt of your pack. Then you can easily check your location on your map when you take an impromptu photo.

We do not recommend laminating maps for your wilderness adventure, since doing so makes it difficult to fold or write on the map.

Finding and Buying Maps

Many outdoor recreation stores and websites sell topographic maps, and some bookstores and nautical supply stores stock them as well.

You can view and order US topographic maps directly from the USGS at store.usgs.gov. There, you can view a PDF version, which you can then enlarge and examine and download for free. If you download topographic maps, then you can print them out on your own printer (see "Printing Your Own Maps," below), or you can bring a digital copy to a local print shop to get a larger hard copy. If you only need a portion of the quadrangle, such as a letter-sized sheet, you can crop the map as desired using PDF software.

To obtain topographic maps for Canada, visit the Natural Resources Canada website at natural-resources.canada.ca and follow prompts to the topographical maps.

Other internet map sources include CalTopo (caltopo.com) for topographic maps of the entire United States, MyTopo (mytopo.com) for the United States and Canada, Canada Topo Maps (canmaps.com/topographic) for Canada, and OpenStreetMap (openstreetmap.org). We recommend purchasing the USGS paper copy directly from the USGS or a commercial map dealer to get the highest-quality map with colorfast ink that will not run when wet. You can also check with local outdoor clubs in your geographic area (e.g., Mazamas, Sierra Club, Colorado Mountain Club, The Mountaineers) to get recommendations for local map sources.

PRINTING YOUR OWN MAPS

Many online map sources allow you to print your own maps at home. If you do this, keep in mind that your software-generated map will only be as good as your printer's capabilities. We recommend using a color laser printer, since the inks used in some inkjet printers are not waterproof, and the colors may run if they get wet. Printing an entire 7.5-minute USGS quadrangle requires nine sheets of 8.5-inch by 11-inch (216 millimeters by 279 millimeters) paper, though you might not need the entire quadrangle at that scale. For example, you might choose to crop your quadrangle and print only the areas of most interest to you at a detailed scale of 1:24,000 or 1:25,000, along with a less detailed (1:100,000 or 1:250,000 scale) map of the larger surrounding area, which may be helpful for approaching your area of interest, for orientation, or for an escape route if required due to accident, illness, or other unexpected change in plans.

Be sure to include a grid of lines on your map; UTM (see chapter 7) is the most useful, particularly if you are also using GPS (see chapter 5). Select WGS 84 as the datum, since this is the default for GPS use. If the printer has a "fit to page" option, turn it off and print it at "100%" or "actual" scale for a true-scale map.

Digital Maps

You can download maps from the USGS website and other online sources and view them on your desktop, tablet, laptop, or smartphone. You can also purchase a small dedicated GPS device that uses preloaded or down-loadable topographic maps. And apps such as CalTopo, Gaia GPS, Back-Country Navigator, Google Maps, and AllTrails all allow you to download maps onto electronic devices (see chapter 5).

If you rely on digital maps for navigation, *you must also carry a backup paper map of the area* to avoid total reliance on an electronic device with limited battery power. Digital maps can become inaccessible when the phone or other device is lost, gets wet or is otherwise damaged, or if its battery is drained. Finally, each member of your party should carry a paper map, so that any member who becomes lost or otherwise separated from the others still has access to a map.

The beauty of studying a map in advance of your journey is that, whether on paper or on an electronic device, you have researched the intended route visually in the comfort of your home. In the process of examining the map for your upcoming trip, you are rehearsing the route of the trip itself. Once en route, you are just executing the route that you have visualized on the map.

You can download maps before you set out and view them on your phone or other electronic device.

CHAPTER SUMMARY

With the exception of your brain, a map is your most important navigational tool. No one should venture into the wilderness without one, nor without the ability to interpret it. You should have ready access to it and consult it frequently during your wilderness adventures.

Fig. 1-11. *Map for chapter 1 Skills Check*

SKILLS CHECK
See the appendix for answers.

1. **What topographic feature is shown at each of the marked points on the map shown in figure 1-11?**

A.	a. steep slope	b. gentle slope	c. nearly flat	d. cliff
B.	a. summit	b. cirque	c. ridge	d. gully
C.	a. cirque	b. ridge	c. gully	d. saddle
D.	a. gentle slope	b. cirque	c. cliff	d. summit
E.	a. steep slope	b. cliff	c. saddle	d. gully
F.	a. ridge	b. gully	c. saddle	d. summit
G.	a. ridge	b. gully	c. saddle	d. summit
H.	a. gully	b. gentle slope	c. summit	d. cliff
I.	a. summit	b. gully	c. steep slope	d. ridge

2. **Identify the elevation in feet for each of the marked points:**

J.	**N.**
K.	**P.**
L.	**Q.**
M.	**R.**

3. **If you are standing at point S and facing uphill, what direction are you facing?**
   a. southeast b. southwest c. northeast d. northwest

4. **If you are standing at point T and facing downhill, what direction are you facing?**
   a. northeast b. southwest c. southeast d. northwest

5. **If you are standing at point U and are facing south, how would you describe the path you are standing on?**
   a. uphill b. downhill c. level

CHECK YOUR ANSWERS. How did you do? If you got all the questions right, then proceed with confidence to the next chapter! If you got some wrong or could not answer some, reread the pertinent sections of this chapter before proceeding on to the next.

CHAPTER 2

COMPASS BASICS

CHAPTER OBJECTIVES

- Learn the types and features of baseplate compasses.
- Cope with magnetic declination.
- Master the four basic steps of using a compass:
  1. Taking (measuring) bearings in the field
  2. Following bearings in the field
  3. Measuring (taking) bearings from a map
  4. Plotting (following) bearings on a map
- Avoid the potential pitfalls of using a compass.
- Practice using a compass.

This chapter lays the foundation for using the compass, as well as for using the map and compass together. Though these principles are easy to learn and apply, they are nevertheless crucial to successful wilderness navigation, so you must study them carefully. If you learn these well, you will become proficient in using the map and compass in the wilderness.

The compass is a very simple device that can do a wondrous thing: it can reveal at any time and any place exactly what direction it is pointing. On a simple wilderness trek in good weather, the compass may never leave your pocket or pack. But as the route becomes more complex or as the weather worsens, or if you are merely curious about identifying various features in your surroundings, it comes into its own as a critical tool of wilderness travel.

A compass is basically a magnetized needle that responds to Earth's magnetic field. Compass makers have added a few things to this basic unit to make it easier to use. But stripped to its core, there is just that needle, aligned with Earth's magnetism, and from that known reference you can determine any other direction.

Types of Baseplate Compasses

The basic features (see fig. 2-1A) of a **baseplate compass** to be used for wilderness travel include:

- A freely rotating magnetic needle—one end is a different color (usually red) from the other so you can tell which end points to north
- A circular, rotating housing, capsule, or **bezel**, for the needle, filled with a fluid that dampens (reduces) the vibrations of the needle, making readings more accurate
- A dial around the circumference of the bezel graduated clockwise in 1- or 2-degree increments, preferably from 0 to 360 degrees (The use of "quadrant" compasses labeled 0° to 90° to 0° to 90° and back to 0° are described in chapter 7, but we do not recommend them, since most guidebooks and references, including this one, utilize the 360-degree method.)
- An orienting arrow or a declination arrow within the capsule, to align with the needle
- A set of parallel meridian lines (also called "orienting lines") located below the needle that rotate with the bezel, separate from the baseplate; these are used to align the compass with meridian (north–south) lines of a map (described in chapter 1)
- A transparent, rectangular baseplate for the entire unit, including a direction-of-travel line (sometimes with an arrow at one end) to point toward your objective; the longer the baseplate, the more accurate your readings will be
- An index line, which is used to set and read bearings, located at the start of the direction-of-travel line
- A ruler or rulers, which are calibrated in inches and/or millimeters, and/ or other scales; these are used to measure short distances or to locate your position on a map

Optional features (see fig. 2-1B) available on some compasses include:

- An adjustable declination arrow instead of a fixed orienting arrow, which is an easy, dependable way to correct for magnetic declination
- A sighting mirror, sometimes with a sighting window and/or a sighting notch—another way to improve accuracy (Compasses with a sighting mirror use the centerline of the mirror as the direction-of-travel line.)

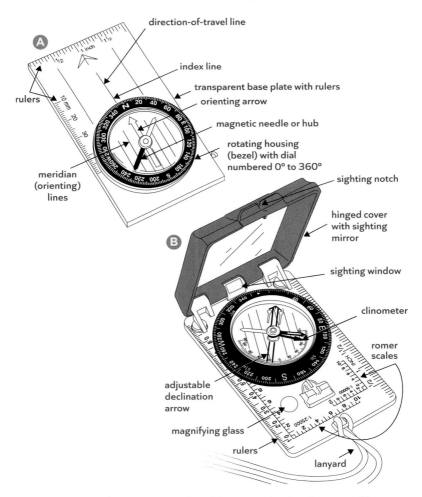

Fig. 2-1. *Features of compasses used in wilderness navigation:* **A,** *essential features;* **B,** *useful optional features*

- A clinometer, used to measure the angle of a slope in the field. Its use is explained in chapter 7.
- A magnifying glass bubble, used to help read closely spaced contour lines and other details on maps
- Romer (sometimes spelled "roamer") scales to enable you to identify your position more precisely on topo maps with UTM lines. If you get a compass without Romer scales, there are several other ways to identify your UTM position on topographic maps (see chapter 7).

"Global" compasses can be used anywhere on Earth. Nonglobal compasses can be affected by compass "dip" if used in another hemisphere than that for which it was made (see chapter 7).

Some compasses have an adjustable declination arrow but no mirror. These cost a little more than the basic compass in figure 2-1A but less than the full-featured compass in figure 2-1B. They are a good value for those who prefer adjustable declination but do not want the added cost and/or weight of the sighting mirror.

The baseplate compasses listed here are the ones we know about as we go to press. By the time the book is available, some of the compasses mentioned here may be discontinued, while still others may appear. But this listing should at least give you an appreciation of the different types of compasses that are available. All the compasses listed have a resolution of 2 degrees unless otherwise noted. Photographs of some typical compasses of each type are shown; these do not necessarily represent the actual compasses in the tables.

> **Tip:** If you purchase a compass with Romer scales, be sure that it has the same scale(s) as your topographic map(s)—for example, 1:24,000 for USGS topographic maps in the United States, and 1:25,000 and/or 1:50,000 for metric maps in Canada, Mexico, and most other countries where the metric system is used.

- **Full-function compasses**: See table 2-1 and figure 2-2. These top-of-the-line compasses have adjustable declination and a sighting mirror, and many have a clinometer. We strongly recommend this type of compass, as they are the best for wilderness navigation. "Gear-driven" declination adjustment is the easiest and most trouble-free; these require a small tool, supplied with the compass.

COMPASS SAFETY

Most compasses have a **lanyard**—a piece of cord a foot (30 centimeters) or longer for attaching the compass to your belt, jacket, or pack. It is not a good idea to put the lanyard around your neck; this is an unsafe practice, particularly when doing any technical climbing, difficult scrambling, or when climbing over and under fallen logs. Some compass manufacturers, aware of this hazard, are now making compasses with a "breakaway" lanyard that breaks off with only a small amount of force, or a detachable lanyard. It is seldom necessary to carry your compass with its lanyard around your neck. If you wish to do so, you might consider purchasing a compass with a breakaway feature.

- **Compasses with adjustable declination but no mirror**: See table 2-2 and figure 2-3. If you do not wish to get a full-function compass, then you should at least get one with adjustable declination, as listed in table 2-2. Note the designation "*adjustable* declination"; this is different from an orienting arrow or a *fixed (nonadjustable) declination scale*, which is a feature of some nonadjustable compasses.
- **Compasses with a mirror but without adjustable declination**: See table 2-3 and figure 2-4. Some people buy this type of compass, mistakenly assuming that since it has a mirror, it must also have adjustable declination. This is not true, and we do not recommend this type. If you already have such a compass and do not wish to replace it, you can modify it for wilderness navigation use as discussed later in this chapter.
- **Minimal compasses**: See table 2-4 and figure 2-5. While these meet all the basic requirements for wilderness travel, they do not have features such as mirrors or adjustable declination, so we do not recommend any of these. If you already have such a compass and do not wish to replace it, you can modify it for wilderness navigation use as discussed later in this chapter.
- **Unacceptable compasses**: Wrist and zipper-pull compasses, those with scales marked in increments (resolution) of 5 degrees or more, and those without rectangular, transparent baseplates are unacceptable.

Table 2-1. FULL-FUNCTION COMPASSES
(with sighting mirror and adjustable declination)

Compass brand and model	Cost (US$)	Romer scales	Magnifier	Breakaway lanyard	Gear-driven declination adjustment	Global	Clinometer	Luminous	Rulers/scales
Silva Ranger 2.0	$$	✔	✔	✔	✔		✔	✔	✔
Silva Expedition S	$$	✔	✔	✔	✔	✔	✔	✔	✔
Suunto MC-2	$$	✔	✔		✔		✔	✔	✔
Suunto MC-2 G	$$$	✔	✔	✔	✔	✔	✔	✔	✔
Brunton TruArc 7	$$					✔	✔		✔
Brunton TruArc 15	$$		✔			✔	✔		✔
Brunton TruArc 15	$$$		✔			✔	✔	✔	✔
Brunton TruArc 20	$$$		✔			✔	✔	✔	✔

$$: $50–75, $$$: $75–99

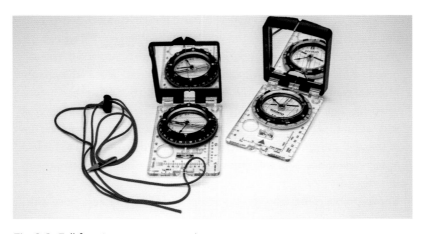

Fig. 2-2. *Full-function compasses*

Table 2-2. COMPASSES WITH ADJUSTABLE DECLINATION BUT NO MIRROR

Compass brand and model	Cost (US$)	Romer scales	Magnifier	Breakaway lanyard	Gear-driven declination adjustment	Global	Clinometer	Luminous	Rulers/scales
Silva Explorer Pro	$$	✔	✔	✔	✔		✔	✔	✔
Suunto M-3	$$		✔	✔	✔			✔	✔
Suunto M-3 G	$$$	✔	✔	✔	✔	✔	✔	✔	✔
Brunton TruArc 5	$				✔				
Brunton TruArc 10	$	✔			✔				✔
Brunton TruArc 10	$$	✔			✔			✔	✔

$: < $50, $$: $50–75, $$$: $75–99

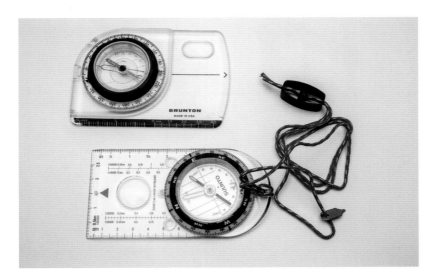

Fig. 2-3. *Compasses with adjustable declination, but no mirror*

Compass brand and model	Cost (US$)	Romer scales	Magnifier	Breakaway lanyard	Fixed (nonadjustable) declination scale	Global (dip)	Clinometer	Luminous	Rulers/scales
Table 2-3. COMPASSES WITH A SIGHTING MIRROR BUT WITHOUT ADJUSTABLE DECLINATION									
Silva Guide 2.0	$			✔	✔			✔	✔
Suunto MCB	$			✔	✔				✔
Suunto Amphibian	$			✔	✔				✔
Silva Guide 426	$			✔	✔				✔

$: < $50

Fig. 2-4. *Compasses with a mirror, but no adjustable declination*

Table 2-4. MINIMAL COMPASSES
(without mirror or adjustable declination)

Compass brand and model	Cost (US$)	Romer scales	Magnifier	Breakaway lanyard	Fixed (nonadjustable) declination scale	Global	Clinometer	Luminous	Rulers/scales
Silva Starter 1-2-3	$				✔				✔
Silva Explorer 2.0	$		✔	✔	✔			✔	✔
Silva Ranger 360 Global	$		✔	✔	✔	✔			✔
Suunto A-10 Partner II	$				✔			✔	✔
Suunto A-15	$		✔		✔			✔	✔
Suunto A-30	$		✔		✔			✔	✔
Sun Company ProMap	$		✔	✔	✔				✔

$: < $50

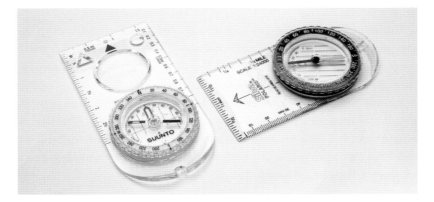

Fig. 2-5. *Minimal compasses*

This includes "lensatic" compasses (see chapter 7). Other unacceptable compasses are those found on smartphones, watches, and GPS devices, since they do not have transparent rectangular baseplates and therefore cannot be used with maps. While they can be handy for quick, approximate direction checks, they cannot be used for precise navigation.

Selecting and Purchasing a Compass

Tables 2-1 through 2-4 contain the features for some of the most widely available compasses. For serious wilderness navigating, we recommend only those shown in tables 2-1 and 2-2. All of these have **adjustable declination**, a feature we consider nearly essential.

The difference between the compasses in table 2-1 and those in table 2-2 is that those in table 2-1 have sighting mirrors, whereas those in table 2-2 do not. The primary advantage of the **mirror** is that most people can obtain more accurate compass readings with a mirrored compass. Furthermore, the mirror effectively doubles the length of the baseplate, thereby making it easier to use to measure and plot bearings on a map. (We will explain the use of the compass mirror later in this chapter.) You can also use the mirror to signal for help in an emergency or use it to ensure complete coverage in the application of sunscreen to your face. If these features are not important to you, then you might consider a compass listed in table 2-2. Most of these are less expensive than those in table 2-1 but have many of the characteristics of a full-featured compass other than the mirror.

The selection of compasses available at outdoor recreation and sporting goods stores is often limited. However, *if you live near such a store, we suggest that you try it first*, since you can then examine the compass carefully and try it out in the store before purchasing it. *Try the declination adjustment feature while in the store and ensure that it functions properly.* If the compass you want is not available at a nearby store, numerous reputable online retailers may have what you are looking for. Returning a defective unit at an online source is not as immediate as returning it to a local store, but you will have a wider selection.

Before purchasing from an online source, be sure to check the company's return policy to ensure that you can easily return a compass that you do not like or that is defective. Read customers' reviews of particular compasses to assess their strengths and weaknesses and to learn of any problems or complaints that others may have encountered with them.

Bearings

A bearing is the direction from one place to another, measured in degrees of angle with respect to an accepted reference line. This reference is the line to true north, also called a **meridian**.

The round dial of a compass is divided into 360 degrees. The direction in degrees to each of the cardinal directions, going clockwise around the dial starting from the top, is north, 0° (also 360°); east, 90°; south, 180°; and west, 270° (see fig. 2-6). The intercardinal directions are northeast (NE), 45°; southeast (SE), 135°; southwest (SW), 225°, and northwest (NW), 315°.

The compass is used for two basic tasks regarding bearings:

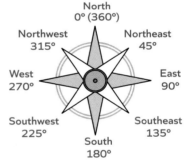

1. *To take, or measure, bearings,* which means to measure the direction from one point to another, either on a map or in the field; the bearing is then read at the index line of the compass

2. *To plot, or follow, bearings,* which means to set a certain bearing at the index line on the compass, and then to plot on the map, or to follow in the field, where that bearing points

Fig. 2-6. *Cardinal and intercardinal directions and corresponding bearings in degrees on the compass*

BEARING AND AZIMUTH

Technically, there is a subtle difference between these two terms, but in conventional modern usage the two terms are often used interchangeably. A **bearing** has traditionally been defined as the angle between either north or south and another direction, measured between 0 and 90 degrees (e.g., S 45° W, meaning 45 degrees west of south). An **azimuth**, on the other hand, is the angle measured clockwise from north, from 0 to 360 degrees (225 degrees in this same example). Many compass manufacturers today, however, define a bearing to be the same as the traditional definition of the azimuth. For example, some compasses have index lines that are marked "read bearing here." In this book, we treat the two as equivalent and refer to them only by the term *bearing*, to be consistent with terminology used by most compass manufacturers.

Bearings in the Field

All bearings in the field are based on where the magnetic needle points. For the sake of simplicity, we will first ignore the effects of magnetic declination, a subject that will be taken up in the next section.

To take (measure) a bearing in the field: Refer to figure 2-7. Hold the compass in front of you and:

1. Point the direction-of-travel line at the object whose bearing you want to find.

2. Rotate the compass housing or bezel until the *pointed end of the orienting or declination arrow is aligned with the north-seeking (usually red) end of the magnetic needle*. (This process is sometimes

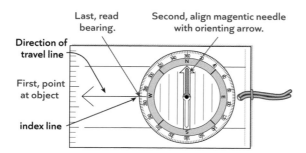

Fig. 2-7. *Taking a compass bearing in the field in an area with zero declination*

referred to as "boxing the needle" or "getting the dog in the doghouse." If you imagine that the pointed end of the arrow looks like the roof of a little shed, you can say "get red in the shed.")

3. Read the bearing at the index line.

Fig. 2-8. *Taking a bearing using a compass that does not have a mirror*

Fig. 2-9. *Taking a bearing using a compass with a mirror*

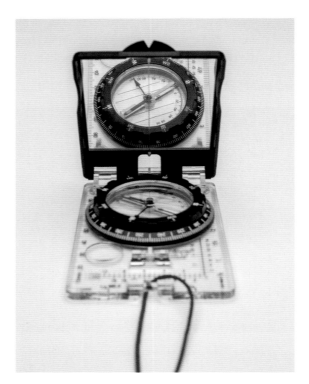

Fig. 2-10. *Close-up of taking a bearing using a compass that has a mirror*

If the compass has no sighting mirror, hold it at or near arm's length and at or near waist level, with your arm straight at about a 45-degree angle from your body (see fig. 2-8). This is a compromise between sighting with the compass at eye level (sighting on your objective along the edge of the compass, without being able to see the compass needle or orienting arrow) and holding it straight down (being able to see the compass needle and arrow without parallax but losing sight of the objective).

With a sighting mirror, no such compromise is necessary. Fold the mirror back to about a 45-degree angle and hold the compass at eye level, with the sight pointing at the object (see fig. 2-9). Observe the magnetic needle and the orienting arrow in the mirror as you rotate the bezel to align the needle and the arrow (see fig. 2-10). The centerline of the mirror should cross the pivot point of the magnetic needle. In either case, hold the compass level. Keep it away from metal objects, which can easily deflect the magnetic needle, giving you a false reading.

To follow (plot) a bearing in the field: Simply reverse the process you used to take a bearing. The same instruction applies whether your compass has a mirror or not:

1. Rotate the compass housing or bezel until you have set the desired bearing at the index line—for example, 270° (west).

2. Hold the compass level in front of you, at roughly arm's length and waist height (as in fig. 2-8). Turn your entire body (including your feet) until the north-seeking (usually red) end of the magnetic needle is aligned with the pointed end of the orienting arrow (i.e., box the needle, or get red in the shed).

3. The direction-of-travel line is now pointing in whatever direction you have set at the index line, in this case west.

When following a bearing, it is best to find some object, such as a big rock or a unique-looking tree, that is in the same direction as the desired bearing. Then put the compass away and walk toward that object until you arrive at it and repeat the process with another visible landmark. This is far safer and faster than walking along, compass in hand, constantly observing the compass, rather than watching where you are going.

Magnetic Declination

A compass needle is attracted to **magnetic north** (presently located in the Arctic Ocean, north of Alaska), while most maps are printed with **true north**—the direction to the geographic North Pole at 90° north latitude—at the top of the map. This difference between the direction to true north and the direction to magnetic north, measured in degrees, is called **magnetic declination**. (Aviators and mariners call this "magnetic variation.") Most compasses will need a simple adjustment or modification to correct for declination.

Magnetic declination varies from place to place and over time. Always use the most current topographic map for your area. To find the amount and direction of declination from the map, look in the lower-left corner on

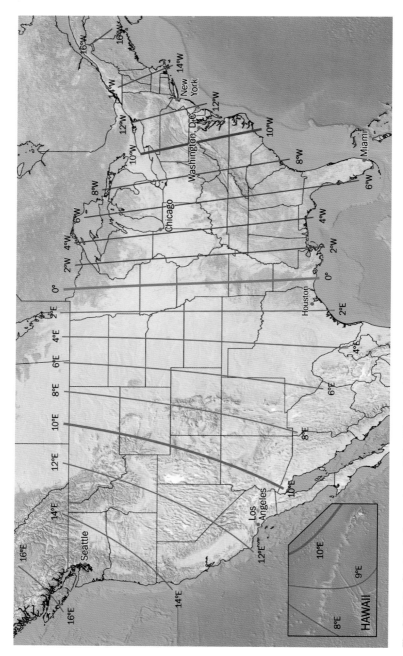

Fig. 2-11. Declination in the contiguous United States and Hawaii in 2025 (Red lines indicate east declination, and blue lines are for west declination. The green line is the agonic line (zero declination).

USGS topographic maps (see fig. 1-7). If the map is more than a few years old, the declination may be somewhat out of date. The maps shown in figures 2-11, 2-12, and 2-13 will give you a fairly close value of the declination in the United States, Mexico and Central America, and Canada. The maps are all adjusted for 2025 and are valid to within 2 degrees for the time interval from 2025 to 2030. (See chapter 7 for information on finding future declinations and for locations outside North America.)

In figure 2-11, you can see that the **line of zero declination** (called the "agonic line") coincidentally runs through parts of Manitoba, Ontario, Minnesota, Iowa, Missouri, Arkansas, and Louisiana at this time. Along this line, the magnetic needle points in the same direction as the geographic North Pole (true north), so *no correction for declination is necessary along the agonic line*.

In areas west of this line, the magnetic needle points somewhere to the east (to the right) of true north, so these areas are said to have **east declination**. It works just the opposite on the other side of the line of zero

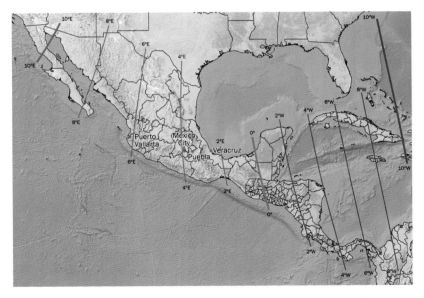

Fig. 2-12. *Declination map for Mexico and Central America in 2025. Red lines indicate east declination, and blue lines are for west declination. The green line is the agonic line (zero declination).*

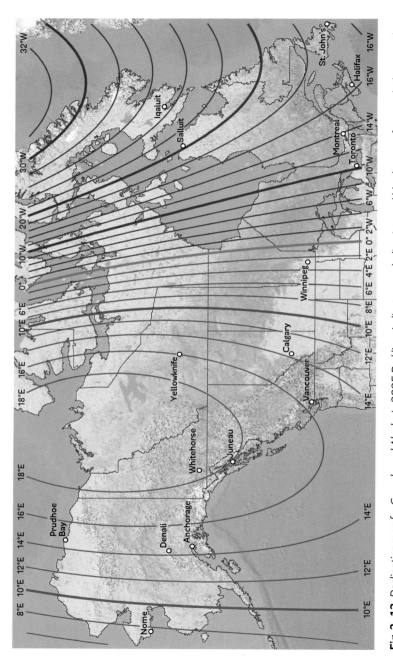

Fig. 2--13. *Declination map for Canada and Alaska in 2025 Red lines indicate east declination, and blue lines are for west declination. The green line is the agonic line (zero declination).*

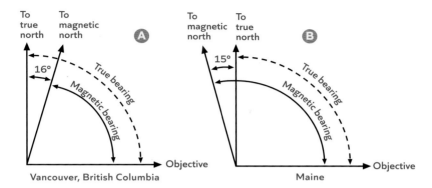

Fig. 2-14. *Magnetic and true bearings:* **A,** *in Vancouver, British Columbia (east declination);* **B,** *in Maine (west declination)*

declination, such as on the East Coast of the United States or Canada. Here, the magnetic needle points somewhere to the west (left) of true north, so these areas are said to have **west declination**.

Consider a traveler near Vancouver, British Columbia, with a declination of 16° east in 2025. The **true bearing** is a measurement of the angle between the line to true north and the line to the objective, as shown in figure 2-14A. The magnetic needle, however, is pulled toward magnetic north, not true north. So the compass measures the angle between the line to magnetic north and the line to the objective. This "magnetic bearing" is 16° less than the true bearing. To get the true bearing, you could add 16° to the magnetic bearing.

As in Vancouver, British Columbia, *travelers in all areas west of the zero-declination line can add the declination to the magnetic bearing to get a true bearing.* In central Colorado, for example, about 8° would be added. In western Utah, it is about 11°.

East of the zero-declination line, the declination can be subtracted from the magnetic bearing to get the true bearing. In central Maine, for example (see fig. 2-14B), the magnetic bearing is about 15° greater than the true bearing. To get a true bearing, the traveler in Maine could subtract the declination of 15° from the magnetic bearing to obtain the true bearing.

This is all very simple in theory but can be confusing in practice, and the wilderness, where a mistake could have serious consequences, is no place

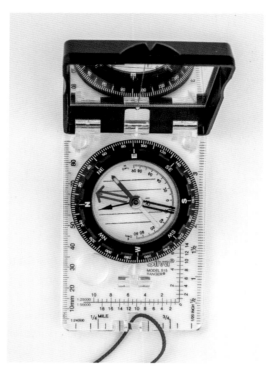

Fig. 2-15. *Adjustable compass set to 16° E declination, as for Vancouver, British Columbia, in 2025*

for mental arithmetic. A more practical way to handle the minor complication of declination is to *pay somewhat more for your compass and get one with an adjustable declination arrow instead of a fixed orienting arrow.* (These are the ones listed in tables 2-1 and 2-2.) By following the instructions supplied with the compass, you can easily set the declination arrow—usually by inserting a tiny screwdriver into a small slot on the bezel and turning it until the declination arrow points at the correct number of degrees east or west of the index line. Then the bearing that you read at the index line will automatically be the true bearing, and concern about a declination error is one worry you can leave at home. Compasses with adjustable declination arrows are sometimes called "set-and-forget" compasses.

If you have a compass with adjustable declination and set it for a declination of 16° E, as for Vancouver, British Columbia, then once properly adjusted, the pointed end of the declination arrow will point to 16° on the bezel, as shown in figure 2-15, and the tail end of the arrow will be at 16° E on the declination scale. In Maine, with a declination of 15° W, the correctly adjusted declination arrow will point to 345° (15° less than 360°), and the tail end of the arrow will be at 15° W on the declination scale.

On compasses without adjustable declination arrows, you can achieve the same effect by sticking a thin strip of adhesive tape to the bottom of the rotating housing or bezel to serve as a customized declination arrow. Trim the tape to a point and apply it to the underside of the compass for the area where you will be traveling, as shown in figure 2-16.

In Vancouver, British Columbia, your taped declination arrow must point at 16° east (clockwise) from the 360° point (marked N for north) on the rotating dial (fig. 2-16A). In Maine, the declination arrow must point at 15° west (counterclockwise) from the 360° mark (fig. 2-16B), or 345°. Note that this taped declination arrow is located in exactly the same place as the adjustable declination arrow described above. Figure 2-17 is a photo of a nonadjustable compass with a taped declination arrow for use in Salluit, Quebec, with a declination of 20° W.

Most nonadjustable compasses have a nonadjustable declination *scale* numbered from 0° to 50° or more, both east and west. You can use this scale to locate the proper position for your taped declination arrow (such as 15° W rather than at 345°). The nonadjustable compass in figure 2-17 illustrates such a declination scale. It is the smaller scale within the center portion of the dial. Some nonadjustable compasses do not have this type of declination scale.

Fig. 2-16. *Compass declination corrections:* **A,** *for an area west of the zero-declination line;* **B,** *for an area east of the zero-declination line*

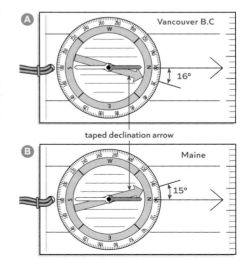

Vancouver B.C

16°

taped declination arrow

Maine

15°

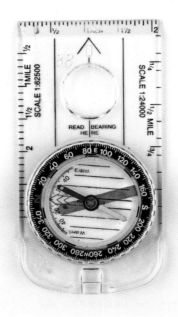

Fig. 2-17. *Nonadjustable compass with taped declination arrow for 20° W declination*

If you travel to an area with a different declination, you will have to change the declination correction. If you have a compass with an adjustable declination arrow, a minor adjustment will allow you to set the compass for the new declination. If you have a taped declination arrow, you will have to peel the tape off and put a new arrow on, to correct for the new declination.

Once your compass is adjusted or modified for the proper declination, you can follow the same procedure to take and follow bearings as used above. The only difference is that, from now on, you will *align the magnetic needle with the declination arrow instead of with the orienting arrow.*

> **Tip:** When using the magnetic needle in the field for taking and following bearings, always remember to align the north-seeking (red) end of the magnetic needle with the "pointed end of the declination arrow to box the needle" or get red in the shed.

From here on we will assume that you are using a compass with a declination arrow—either an adjustable declination arrow or a taped arrow that you have added. *For all bearings in the field, you will align the needle with this declination arrow.* All compass bearings used from this point on are true bearings. We will not refer to magnetic bearings again, since we always automatically convert all bearings to true ones using one of the two techniques described above.

Back Bearings

A **back bearing** (also called "back azimuth" or "reciprocal bearing") is the opposite direction of a bearing. Back bearings are often useful when you are trying to follow a certain bearing, and you want to check to see if you are still on the bearing line by taking a back bearing on your starting point. If your original bearing is less than 180°, then you can find the back bearing by adding 180° to the original bearing. If your original bearing is greater than 180°, then you can find the back bearing by subtracting 180° from the original bearing. For example, if you are traveling at a bearing of 90°, then the back bearing is 270°. Once you reach your

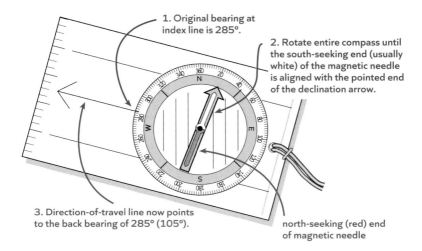

1. Original bearing at index line is 285°.

2. Rotate entire compass until the south-seeking end (usually white) of the magnetic needle is aligned with the pointed end of the declination arrow.

3. Direction-of-travel line now points to the back bearing of 285° (105°).

north-seeking (red) end of magnetic needle

Fig. 2-18. *Finding a back bearing using a compass*

destination, following the back bearing of 270° should get you back to your starting point.

We previously mentioned that we do not recommend mental arithmetic in the wilderness, since it is too easy to make mistakes. A better way of working with a back bearing is to keep the original bearing at the index line and rotate the compass until the **south-seeking end** (usually white, but sometimes black) of the magnetic needle is aligned with the pointed end of the declination arrow, as shown in figure 2-18. The use of back bearings in wilderness navigation will be described in more detail in chapter 3.

Bearings on a Map

You can use your compass as a protractor, both to measure and to plot bearings on a map. Magnetic north and magnetic declination have nothing to do with these operations. Therefore, *ignore the magnetic needle when measuring or plotting bearings on a map.* (The only time you need to use the magnetic needle when working with the map is whenever you choose to orient the map to true north, which we will explain in chapter 3. But there is no need to orient the map to measure or plot bearings.)

To measure a bearing on a map (see fig. 2-19):

1. Place the compass on the map with one long edge of the baseplate running between the two points of interest. To measure the bearing from point A to point B, make sure that the direction-of-travel line is pointing parallel to the direction from A to B (not the reverse).

2. Turn the rotating housing (bezel) until the compass meridian (or orienting) lines are parallel to the meridian (north–south) lines of the map. Be sure that the N on the compass dial is toward the top of the map and that the S is toward the bottom. (If you put the N toward the bottom of the map, with the S toward the top, your reading will be 180 degrees off.) For the utmost in accuracy, slide the compass along the bearing line so that one of its meridian (orienting) lines is exactly on top of one of the north–south lines on the map.

3. Read the number that is at the index line. This is the bearing from point A to point B.

Example: Suppose you are at the summit of Panic Peak and you want to know which of the many peaks around you is Deception Dome. Your map shows both peaks (fig. 2-19), so you can measure the bearing on the map from point A, Panic Peak, to point B, Deception Dome. The result, as read at the index line, is 34°. (In this figure, we have purposely omitted the magnetic needle for the sake of clarity, and because it is not used here.) You can then hold the compass out in front of you and turn your entire body until you box the needle. The direction-of-travel line will then point toward Deception Dome and you can identify it.

What about plotting a bearing on your map? In this case you are starting with a known bearing. And where does that bearing come from? From an actual landscape compass reading. For example, your friend returns from a backpacking trip, remorseful for having left a camera somewhere along the trail. While at a rest stop, your friend took a photo, and at the

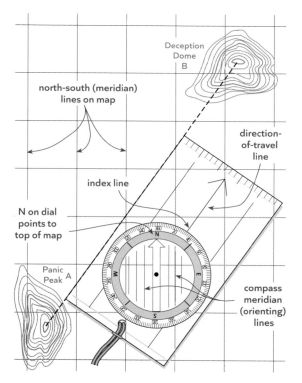

Fig. 2-19.
Measuring a bearing on a map with the compass as a protractor (magnetic needle omitted for clarity)

same spot had taken a bearing on Mount Magnificent and found it to be 130°. That is all you need to know. You are heading into that same area next weekend, so you get out the Mount Magnificent quadrangle. To plot a bearing on your map (see fig. 2-20):

1. First set the bearing of 130° at the compass index line. Place the compass on the map, one long edge of the baseplate touching the summit of Mount Magnificent.

2. Rotate the entire compass (not just the bezel) until the meridian (orienting) lines in the compass bezel are parallel with the map's meridian (orienting) lines. Make sure that the edge of the baseplate is still touching the summit. Again, make sure that the N on the compass dial is toward the top of the map.

3. Draw a line along the edge of the baseplate. Where this line crosses the trail is where your friend's camera is (or was).

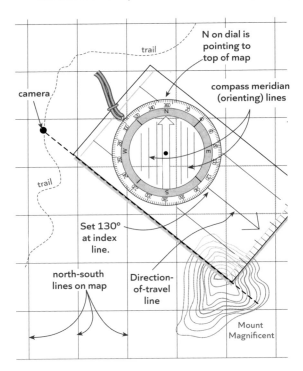

Fig. 2-20. *Plotting a bearing on a map with the compass as a protractor (magnetic needle omitted for clarity)*

When measuring or plotting bearings on a map, the map does not need to be in a horizontal position, such as lying down on the snow or dirt, on a stump, or in the mud. Instead, it can be vertical or in any other position. Its orientation doesn't matter, since you are just using the compass as a protractor.

In the forest, you can place the compass up against a tree to do the map-and-compass work. On a snowfield or glacier, with no trees, you can instead ask another member of the party to stand still while you steady the map against the person's pack or back. Or you can sit down on your pack and do the map work in your lap or on your knee with your legs crossed.

Practicing with a Compass

Before you count on your compass skills in the wilderness, be sure to test them in an area near your home. The best place to practice is where you already know all the answers, such as at a street intersection where the roads run north–south and east–west.

- Take a bearing in a direction you know to be east. When you have pointed the direction-of-travel line at something that you know is east of you, such as along the edge of the street or sidewalk or curb, and have boxed the needle, the number at the index line should be very close to 90 degrees.
- Repeat for the other cardinal directions: south, west, and north (see fig. 2-6). Then try all four again to see how repeatable the bearings are.
- Try to refine your technique to improve your accuracy. You may have to hold the compass higher or lower, or perhaps close one eye. Find out how accurate you can be. After some practice, you should consistently be able to get to within 2 degrees of the correct bearing. This is usually adequate. (If you cannot achieve this level of accuracy, or if you need better accuracy, you can get an optical sighting compass, described in chapter 7).
- Then try the reverse process. Pretend you do not know which way is west. Set 270° at the index line and hold the compass out in front of you as you turn your entire body (including your feet) until the needle is boxed. The direction-of-travel line should now point west. Does it?
- Repeat for the other three cardinal directions.

This set of exercises will help you to develop your skills and self-confidence related to using compasses and is also a way to check the accuracy of your compass. And if you make a mistake or two, no harm done.

You can practice measuring and plotting bearings on a map using the examples shown in figures 2-19 and 2-20. These figures are drawn with the correct angular proportions, so if you place your compass on the page, you should get the same answers we get.

If you ever doubt the accuracy of your compass—perhaps because it has developed a small bubble or has given you a questionable reading in the field—take it out to the street intersection again to test it. If the bearings you read are more than a few degrees away from the correct ones, consider replacing your compass. (Compass needles can sometimes become demagnetized, or their magnetic orientation can even reverse, if the compass is stored in areas with strong electric or magnetic fields.)

Look for places to practice in the wilderness. A good place is any known location (e.g., a summit or a lakeshore) from which you can identify your exact position and can see identifiable landmarks. Take bearings on some of these and plot them on the map to see how close the result is to your actual location.

DOES YOUR BEARING MAKE SENSE?

Whenever you measure or plot bearings on a map, it is a good idea to first guess at the answer based on visual observations, common sense, and your knowledge of the cardinal directions. Then if the bearing you carefully measure or plot is nowhere near your original guess, you may have made one of those 180° errors previously mentioned.

For example, suppose you want to measure a bearing on a map, and this bearing is somewhere between northeast (45°) and east (90°). You might guess that it is 50° to 80° or so. Then suppose you measure the bearing as accurately as possible using your compass with the map. You line up one of the compass meridian lines exactly on top of one of the map's north–south lines, getting the bearing accurate to the nearest degree, and the number you read at your index line is 247°. Does this agree with your original guess? No! You must have made one of those 180° mistakes, and the correct answer is 67°.

Tips and Cautions for Compass Use

There is a big difference between using a compass for working with a map and using a compass for fieldwork. In the field, you must box the needle by aligning the pointed end of the declination arrow with the red end of the magnetic needle. When measuring and plotting bearings on a map, however, you ignore the compass needle. Just align the meridian (orienting) lines in the compass housing with the north–south lines on the map, with the N of the compass dial toward north on the map. In both cases, the direction-of-travel line must point from you to your objective (not the reverse).

You may have heard that nearby metal can mess up a compass bearing. This is true. Ferrous objects such as iron and steel deflect the magnetic needle and give false readings. Keep the compass away from belt buckles, ice axes, and other metal objects. Some wristwatches, particularly digital ones, can also cause false readings if they are too close to the compass. Large electrical currents, such as those in nearby powerlines, can induce electromagnetic fields that can also disrupt compass bearings. If a compass reading does not make sense, see if nearby metal or electricity is sabotaging your bearing.

Keep your wits about you when pointing the direction-of-travel line and the declination arrow. If you point either of them backward—an easy thing to do—the reading will be 180 degrees off. If the bearing is north, the compass will say it is south. Remember that the north-seeking end of the magnetic needle must be aligned with the pointed end of the declination arrow and that the direction-of-travel line must point from you to your objective.

When taking and following bearings in the field, you can also begin by making an intelligent guess at the result, then use the compass to get the exact answer. Before blindly following the compass, you can then ask yourself if the result from the compass agrees with your rough guess and common sense.

When traveling in sunshine, you should be able to at least roughly check your compass readings by noting the position of the Sun in the sky, since it always rises in the eastern (or northeastern or southeastern) sky, is due south at midday, and sets in the western (or northwestern or southwestern) sky. This is very approximate, but it is close enough to detect a 180° error.

Map and Compass: A Checklist

So, do you have the hang of using a compass? There are four essential compass operations that you must learn: taking and following bearings in the field, and measuring and plotting bearings on the map. Let us summarize these one last time. Check off each operation as you do it.

TO TAKE A BEARING IN THE FIELD

☐ Hold the compass level, in front of you. Point the direction-of-travel line at the desired object.

☐ Rotate the compass housing or bezel to align the pointed end of the declination arrow with the red end of the magnetic needle (box the needle or get red in the shed).

☐ Read the bearing at the index line.

TO FOLLOW A BEARING IN THE FIELD

☐ Set the desired bearing at the index line.

☐ Hold the compass level, in front of you. Turn your entire body, including your feet, until the red end of the magnetic needle is aligned with the pointed end of the declination arrow (box the needle or get red in the shed).

☐ Travel in the direction shown by the direction-of-travel line.

TO MEASURE A BEARING ON A MAP

☐ Refer to figure 2-19. Place the compass on the map, with one long edge of the baseplate joining two points of interest. The direction-of-travel line points to your objective.

☐ Rotate the housing to align the compass meridian lines with the north–south lines on the map, with N on the compass toward the top of the map.

☐ Read the bearing at the index line.

TO PLOT A BEARING ON A MAP

☐ Refer to figure 2-20. Set the desired bearing at the index line.

☐ Place the compass on the map, with one long edge of the baseplate on the feature from which you wish to plot the bearing.

☐ Turn the entire compass to align its meridian lines with the map's north–south lines, with N on the compass toward the top of the map. The edge of the baseplate is now on the bearing line.

Whenever you perform any of these operations, first guess at the answer, and then perform the operation as accurately as you can. Finally, compare your answer to your original guess to ensure that you are not making a 180° error. Ensure that your answer makes sense to you.

If in doubt, trust your compass. The compass, correctly used, is almost always right, while your contrary judgment may be clouded by fatigue, confusion, or hurry. If you get a nonsensical reading, check to see if perhaps you are making a 180° error. If not, and if no metal or electricity is nearby, verify the reading with other members of the party, using different compasses. If they get the same answer, trust your compass over hunches, blind guesses, and intuition.

CARRYING YOUR COMPASS

It is a good idea to carry your compass in a place that is readily accessible, so that you can easily and quickly check your compass without taking off your pack. Carrying your compass in a cargo pocket will accomplish this. If it is inconvenient to get to your compass, it is unlikely that you will use it when you should.

A Final Reminder

- When taking and following bearings in the field, always align the pointed end of the declination arrow with the north-seeking (red) end of the magnetic needle (box the needle or get red in the shed).
- Never use the magnetic needle or the declination arrow when measuring or plotting bearings on the map. Just make sure that the N on the compass dial is toward north on the map, not south, as a check to ensure that the compass meridian lines are not upside-down.

Once you master these four essential operations with the compass, you will have all the basic knowledge you need for map-and-compass orientation, navigation, and routefinding. The remainder of this book is based on these operations. If you thoroughly understand how to do them, you can proceed through the rest of the book with confidence, and you will easily understand everything that we explain.

If you are unsure of any of these four operations, we suggest that you stop now and reread this chapter. Study it carefully. Do the simple street-corner compass exercises that were described for taking and following bearings. Measure and plot the bearings shown in figures 2-19 and 2-20. You must thoroughly understand each of these operations before proceeding with the rest of this book. Finally, perform the Skills Check exercises below to verify your knowledge of these operations.

See chapter 7 for more information on changing declination, using a clinometer, and some other types of compasses, or if you ever plan to travel to foreign lands on distant continents, where you may not know the declination or where the compass may be adversely affected by magnetic dip.

CHAPTER SUMMARY

This chapter covered different types and characteristics of compasses, what they do, how they work, and how to use a compass to take and follow bearings in the field, and to measure and plot bearings on a map. You have also been given tips and suggestions for practicing compass use and avoiding commonly made mistakes when using a compass.

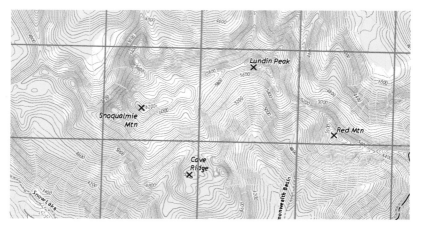

Fig. 2-21. *Map for chapter 2 Skills Check*

SKILLS CHECK

See the appendix for answers.

1. **If your magnetic bearing is 253° and your declination is 10° W, what is your true bearing?**

   a. 263°   b. 243°   c. 83°   d. 63°

2. **If your magnetic bearing is 124° and your declination is 10° E, what is your true bearing?**

   a. 314°   b. 294°   c. 134°   d. 114°

3. **If your true bearing is 224° and your declination is 20° E, what is your magnetic bearing?**

   a. 24°   b. 204°   c. 244°   d. 64°

4. **If your true bearing is 273° and your declination is 20° W, what is your magnetic bearing?**

   a. 113°   b. 253°   c. 73°   d. 293°

5. **Give the values in degrees for northeast (NE), southwest (SW), southeast (SE), and northwest (NW).**

   a. NE: b. SW: c. SE: d. NW:

6. **Using the magnetic declination maps given in this chapter, determine the magnetic declination to the nearest degree for the year 2025 for the following locations:**

   a. New York, NY: b. Chicago, IL: c. Los Angeles, CA:

   d. Honolulu, HI: e. Juneau, AK: f. Nome, AK:

7. **In the map shown on figure 2-21, what is the true bearing from Cave Ridge to Red Mountain?**

8. **What is the true bearing from Lundin Peak to Cave Ridge?**

9. **Plot a true bearing of 310° from Red Mountain. What mountain peak does it go through?**

10. **Plot a true bearing of 140° from Snoqualmie Mountain. What mountain peak does it go to?**

CHECK YOUR ANSWERS. How did you do? If you got all the questions right, then proceed with confidence to the next chapter! If you got some wrong or could not answer some, reread the pertinent sections of this chapter before proceeding on to the next.

CHAPTER 3

ORIENTATION & NAVIGATION

CHAPTER OBJECTIVES

- Master the science of orientation, first by keeping track of your position through awareness and observation.
- Learn the meaning of *point, line,* and *area position.*
- Learn how to orient a map with your surroundings.
- Learn the advantages of using the bearing of the slope.
- Learn the principles of terrain navigation by following natural topographic features.
- Learn how to find the route to a distant objective using a map and compass.
- Follow a route using a compass alone.
- Make use of *aiming off* (an intentional offset).
- Cope with the special problem of the parallel path.
- Learn techniques for navigating around an obstruction.
- Know the importance of maintaining awareness of where you are and where you are headed.

Orientation

Figuring out your exact location is usually relatively simple: just look around and compare what you see with what is on your map. However, sometimes this is not accurate enough, or there is nothing much nearby to identify on the map. The usual solution then is to get out your compass and to try for bearings on some landscape features, or to get out your GPS device. This is **orientation by instrument**. But before resorting to this, first study the map carefully to see if there are any topographic features—even subtle ones—that you can associate with the landscape around you. *If you have been carefully observing your map and comparing it with the landscape—and keeping track of your location on the map (continually orienting yourself), as we suggested in chapter 1—you should always have a fairly good idea of where you are.* Orientation by instrument should be reserved for those situations in which nothing else works, for compass practice, or for verifying your location after using other methods.

The goal of orientation is to determine that precise point on Earth's surface where you now stand. You can represent your position by a mere dot on the map. This is known as **point position**.

There are two lower levels of orientation. One is called **line position**: you know you are along a certain line on a map—such as a river, trail, ridge, compass bearing, or contour line—but you do not know where you are along that line.

The lowest level of orientation is **area position**: you know the general area you are in, but that is all. The objective of orientation is to determine your exact point position.

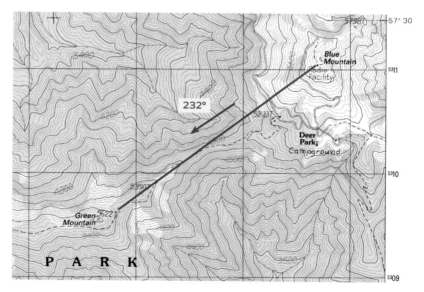

Fig. 3-1. *Example of point position*

POINT POSITION

With point position known, you know exactly where you are, and you can use that knowledge to identify on the map any major feature that you can see in the landscape. You can also identify in the landscape any major visible feature that is shown on the map. Knowing your point position is an essential first step in navigation.

Example: Suppose you have hiked to the summit of Blue Mountain (fig. 3-1). You know your point position: the top of Blue Mountain. You see an unknown peak and want to know what it is. You take a compass bearing on it and get 232°. You plot 232° from Blue Mountain on your map, and the plotted line passes through Green Mountain. The unknown peak is Green Mountain. However, if you want to determine which of the many peaks around you is Green Mountain, you must do the map work first. You measure the bearing on the map from where you are—Blue Mountain—to Green Mountain and get 232°. Keeping the 232° at the index line, turn the entire compass until the needle is boxed. The direction-of-travel line then points toward Green Mountain.

LINE POSITION

Once you know line position, the goal is to determine point position. If you know that you are on a trail, ridge, or some other easily identifiable line, you need only one more trustworthy piece of information to get your point position.

Example: Suppose a party of scramblers is on Unsavory Ridge (fig. 3-2), but they do not know exactly where they are on the ridge. In the distance is Mount Magestic, and a bearing on it indicates 220°. They plot 220° from Mount Majestic on the map and run this line back toward Unsavory Ridge. Where it intersects the ridge is where the scramblers are.

AREA POSITION

If you only know your general area, you need at least two trustworthy pieces of information to determine your point position.

Example: Suppose some snowshoers know they are in the general area of Fantastic Crags (fig. 3-3), their area position. They want to determine line position and then, from that, point position. They may be able to

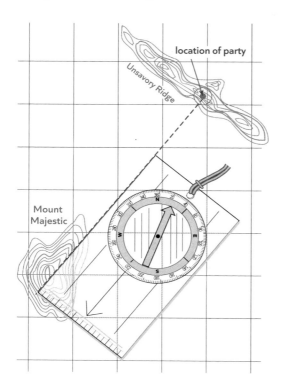

Fig. 3-2. *Orientation with line position known (magnetic needle omitted for clarity)*

location of party

Unsavory Ridge

Mount Majestic

use bearings on two known, recognizable features. They take a bearing on Fantastic Peak and get a reading of 40°. They plot a line on the map, along the baseplate and through Fantastic Peak, at 40°. They know they must be somewhere on or near that bearing line, so they now have line position. They can also see Unsavory Spire. A bearing on the spire shows 130°. They plot this line on the map, through Unsavory Spire, and draw a line along the baseplate. The two bearing lines intersect, and that is their location—or approximately so.

Whenever you take a bearing in the field or plot a bearing on a map, it is inevitable that minor errors will creep in to create larger errors in the estimate of your position. It is very easy to make an error of 3 degrees in taking a bearing, and another 2 degrees in plotting that bearing, unless you are extremely careful. For every 5 degrees of error, your position will be in error by about 460 feet in every mile (about 90 meters in every kilometer). If you take and plot a bearing on a landmark 3 miles (5 kilometers) away, and make a 5-degree error, the plotted line could be about 1400 feet (430 meters) away from the correct position. Therefore, *be sure that your conclusions agree with common sense.* If you take and plot bearings from two peaks and find that the two lines intersect in the middle of a river, but you are standing on a high point of land, something is wrong. Try again. Try to take a more accurate bearing, and plot it more carefully. If bearing lines intersect at a map location with no similarity to the terrain, you may have errors in your bearings. Or there might be some magnetic anomaly in the rocks, or you might have an inaccurate map. And who knows? Maybe those peaks are not really the peaks you think they are. Make sure that the two bearings are not from approximately the same direction, since this can

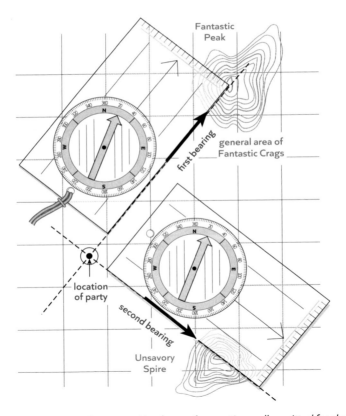

Fig. 3-3. *Orientation with area position known (magnetic needle omitted for clarity)*

compound any error. *The closer an angle of intersection is to 90 degrees, the more accurate the point position will be.*

The technique of *taking and plotting bearings from landmarks is more accurate if you can see three landmarks* and plot three bearings. The result will be a small triangle (called a "cocked hat," see fig. 3-4). Your position is most likely within this triangle. The size of the triangle will also give you an estimate of the accuracy of your compass readings and line plotting.

Orienting a Map

During a wilderness excursion it sometimes helps to hold the map in a traditional manner so that north on the map is pointed in the actual direction of true north. This is known as orienting the map, a good way to obtain a better feel of the relationship between the map and the countryside.

One way to orient a map is *by inspection*: simply look at the terrain and compare it to the map. Then hold the map level and turn it until the map is lined up with the terrain.

However, often this technique will not work because you cannot see any identifiable features around you. In this case, you can orient your map

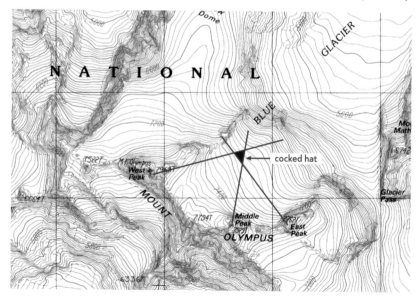

Fig. 3-4. *Plotting three bearings results in a "cocked-hat" position.*

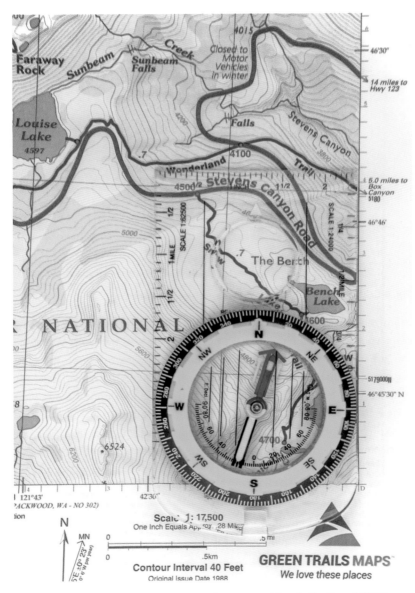

Fig. 3-5. *Using a compass to orient a map in an area with a declination of 15° E: Note how 360° (N) on the compass dial is aligned with geographic north (N) on the map, and the magnetic needle is aligned with magnetic north (MN) on the map. The map is now oriented.*

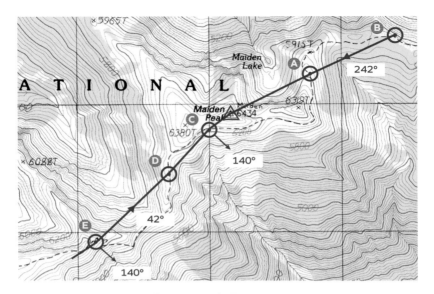

Fig. 3-6. *Using the bearing of the slope to find your position*

using your compass. Set 360° (north) at the index line of the compass and place your compass on the map. Put one long edge of the baseplate along the left or right edge of the map as shown in figure 3-5, with the N of the compass dial pointing to the direction of north on the map. Then hold the map level and turn the map and compass together until the needle is boxed. The map is now oriented to the scene around you. (Map orientation can give you a general feel for the area, but it cannot replace the more precise methods of orientation that we covered in the preceding chapter.)

Direction and Bearing of the Slope

You can often find your position by using the **direction of the slope**, which was first described in chapter 1 using general directions such as east or southwest. This technique can be refined by using the more precise **bearing of the slope**. For example, suppose you are hiking along the trail near Maiden Peak (fig. 3-6) and want to find your point position. You take a bearing on Maiden Peak and get 242°. You plot this bearing and find that it crosses the trail in two places, A and B. Where are you? Points A and B are both on a ridge, but at point A the slope falls off to the east, while at point B it falls off to the north. Suppose you take your compass and point it in the direction of the slope. You find that the actual slope falls off to the north. That tells you that you are at point B, not point A.

Sometimes the situation is a little more subtle, so you need more accuracy with this approach. In this case, you should refer to the bearing of the slope rather than merely its general direction. Imagine that another party is also on the Maiden Peak Trail and wants to find its position. They take a bearing on Maiden Peak and get 42°. They plot this line, as shown in figure 3-6, and they see that the bearing line crosses the trail in three places. Where are they: point C, D, or E? A quick compass bearing shows that the slope falls off roughly to the southeast, so point D is ruled out, since at that point the map clearly shows the slope to fall off to the east. That narrows it down to either point C or point E. A party member faces downhill and takes a more careful bearing in the direction of the fall line. Suppose the bearing is 140°. One long edge of the compass is then placed on the map at point C, and the entire compass is rotated until the meridian lines in the compass housing are parallel with the meridian lines on the map, with the N on the compass dial toward the top of the map. The edge of the baseplate should then point in a direction perpendicular to the contour lines at point C. However, you can see that the bearing of 140° is *not* perpendicular to the contour lines at point C. Thus the same process can be repeated for point E. This time, the bearing line is nearly perpendicular to the contour lines, at least for the first 200 feet down from point E. From this, they conclude that they are at point E.

Situational Awareness

If you ignore cues from the terrain, your situational awareness is diminished, which directly affects your safety. Fight this tendency with several techniques. Start by observing your surroundings and updating your mental map of the landscape. Correlate your surroundings with the physical map. Study myriad details around you, including slope, sun position, ridges, and terrain features, and confirm them using your altimeter and compass. Then decide on your next steps. Maintain your heightened sense of situational awareness by repeating this **observe-orient-decide-act cycle** while you move through the landscape.

The best method of orientation is to *use your map and your continual observations of topography to keep track of where you are.* Presumably, at the beginning of your trek you know where you are and can identify that position on the map. If you then follow your progress on the map, noting each topographic or other feature that you pass along the way, then at any time you should know your position with a great amount of certainty.

Navigation by Instrument

Now that you have learned the fundamentals of orientation, you can determine exactly where you are. You can then determine the direction to travel to get to your desired destination: the process of navigation. This section will explain a variety of methods to do so.

Getting from here to there is usually just a matter of keeping an eye on the landscape and watching where you are going, helped by an occasional glance at the map. However, if you cannot see your objective in the field, you can measure the bearing on the map, then take compass in hand and follow the direction-of-travel line as it guides you to your goal. This is **navigation by instrument**. It is a technique that will work if you are able to follow a straight-line route, something often impossible in wilderness terrain. For this reason, it is best to first try to follow trails or topographic features in wilderness navigation, and reserve navigation by instrument for those situations where the topography lacks sufficient features to be of any help to you.

Navigation by instrument is sometimes the only practical method for finding a crucial pass, base camp, or other goal. It also serves as a supplement to other methods, such as following topographic features, and it can help to verify that you are on the right track. Again, use common sense, and challenge a compass reading that defies reason. (Is your declination arrow or direction-of-travel line pointing the wrong way, sending you 180 degrees off course?)

MAP AND COMPASS NAVIGATION

The most common situation requiring instrument navigation comes when the route is unclear because the topography is featureless or because landmarks are obscured by forest or fog. You know exactly where you are and exactly where you want to go, and you can identify both your present position and your destination on the map. In this case, simply measure the

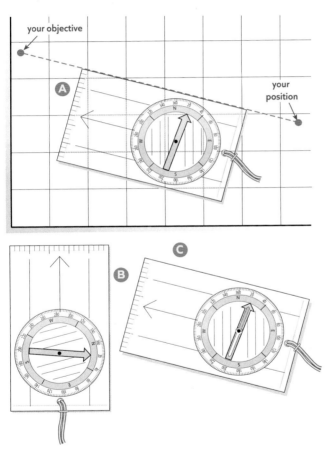

Fig. 3-7. *Navigation using a map and compass:* **A,** *measuring the bearing on the map from your position to your destination (magnetic needle omitted for clarity);* **B,** *reading the bearing at the index line (leave the compass set; magnetic needle omitted for clarity);* **C,** *following the bearing*

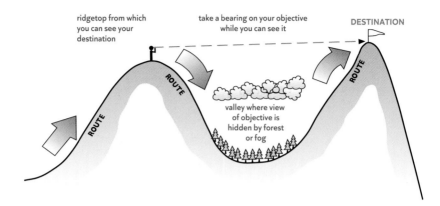

Fig. 3-8. *Following a compass bearing when the view of the objective is obscured by forest or fog*

bearing from your present position to your objective on the map, and then follow that bearing to your objective.

Example: Suppose you measure a bearing of 285° on the map (fig. 3-7A). Note that the north–south (orienting) lines in the compass housing are parallel with the north–south (meridian) lines on the map, with the N on the compass dial aligned with the top of the map. Read this bearing at the index line and leave it set there (fig. 3-7B). Then hold your compass out in front of you as you rotate your body until you have boxed the needle. The direction-of-travel line now points to your objective (fig. 3-7C). Start walking.

COMPASS ALONE

Navigators of air and ocean often travel by instrument alone; you can too. For example, suppose you are scrambling toward a ridgetop and clouds begin to obscure your view. Just take a quick compass bearing on the destination before it disappears from view, then follow that bearing, compass in hand if you wish. You do not even have to note the numerical bearing; just box the needle and keep it boxed as you proceed to your objective. Likewise, if you are heading into a valley where fog or forest will hide your destination, take a bearing on that goal before you drop into the valley, and then follow that bearing after you lose sight of the objective (fig. 3-8). This

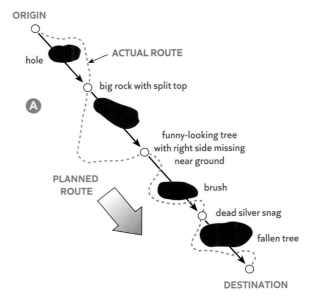

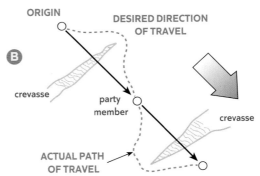

Fig. 3-9. *Use of intermediate objectives:* **A,** *in the forest;* **B,** *on a glacier*

method becomes more reliable if several people travel together, checking each other's work by taking occasional back bearings on each other.

INTERMEDIATE OBJECTIVES

For those frustrating times when you try to travel exactly along a compass bearing but are frequently diverted by obstructions such as cliffs, dense brush, or crevasses, try the technique of **intermediate objectives**. If in a forest, sight past the obstruction to a tree, rock, or other object that is exactly on the bearing line to the principal objective (fig. 3-9A). Then you are free to travel over to the tree or rock by whatever route is easiest. When you get to the intermediate objective, you can be confident that you are still on the correct route. This technique is useful even when there is no obstruction. Moving from one intermediate objective to another means you can put the compass away for those stretches, rather than having to hold it continuously in your hand and check it every few steps.

Sometimes on snow or glaciers, in fog, or in a forest where all the trees look the same, there may be no natural intermediate objectives. In this case, another member of the party can serve as the target (fig. 3-9B). Send that

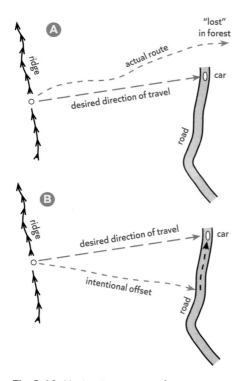

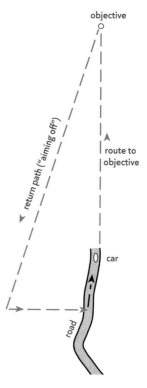

Fig. 3-10. *Navigating to a specific point on a line:* **A,** *Inevitable minor errors can sometimes have disastrous consequences;* **B,** *To avoid such problems, follow a course with an intentional offset.*

Fig. 3-11. *Example of traveling on a path parallel to a road, trail, or other line position*

person out to near the limit of visibility or past the obstruction. Wave that person left or right until he or she is directly on the bearing line. That person can improve the accuracy of the route by taking a back bearing on you.

THE INTENTIONAL OFFSET ("AIMING OFF")

Now imagine that your party is almost back to the car after a scramble. You follow a compass bearing to the logging road, but you cannot see the car because you are off route by a few degrees. You have to guess which way to go. It is a bad ending to the trip if the car is to the right and you go left. It will be even worse if the car is parked at the end of the road, and a routefinding error takes the party beyond that point and on and on through the woods (fig. 3-10A). The **intentional offset** (also called "aiming off") was invented for this situation (fig. 3-10B). Just travel in a direction that is intentionally offset by 20 to 30 degrees to the right of wherever you want to be. When you hit the road, there will be no doubt about which way to turn.

THE PARALLEL PATH

One of the most vexing navigational problems can be the situation you encounter when you are traveling in a direction that parallels the direction of a road, trail, or other feature to which you must return in order to get back home. Such a situation is illustrated in figure 3-11. A party drives along a fairly straight road to its end, parks the car, and hikes to their objective in a direction exactly parallel to the road. Both the road and the objective are clearly visible on the map, so once at the objective the party can follow the back bearing to the road end. When following this bearing back, however, it might not be possible to stay exactly on route, due to irregularities in the topography. Consequently, when the party nears the car, they may have missed the end of the road and ended up in the woods to either the right or the left of the road.

With a little forethought, they could have avoided this situation by using a variation of the aiming-off technique. In this example in figure 3-11, they could have purposely taken a route 20 to 30 degrees to the right of the correct path, to a point safely past the end of the road. Once sure they were past this point, they could then turn sharply toward the road, and they would soon intersect it. A short hike up the road would then lead them back to the car. The overall trip would be longer than if they had taken a direct path, but the latter might have caused them to miss the road entirely. It is easier to head for a large-angle objective such as a road, stream, or trail than to attempt to find a precise point such as the end of a road.

NAVIGATING AROUND AN OBSTRUCTION

Sometimes you may try to follow a constant bearing to get to your objective but find that the route is blocked by an obstruction such as a lake or

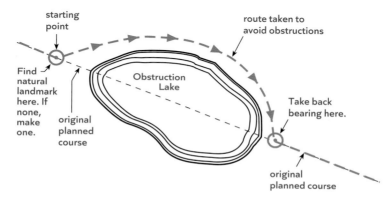

Fig. 3-12. *Navigating around an obstruction when you can see across it once you are past it*

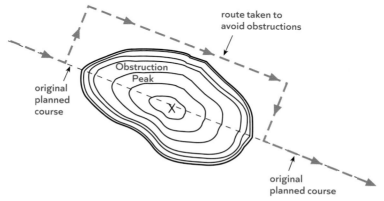

Fig. 3-13. *Navigating around an obstruction when the view across it is blocked*

cliff. There may be an easy way to get around the obstruction, but doing so forces you off your intended bearing. What do you do to stay on the correct bearing?

If the obstruction is a lake or swamp, you may be able to see across it back to your starting point after you have traveled past it (fig. 3-12). In this case, *try to find some large, easily visible object on your bearing line before you start traveling past the obstruction.* If that point is a nonde-script location with no identifiable landmark, you can mark this spot by building a pile of fallen logs or some other temporary landmark that you will be able to see from the other side of the obstruction. (See "Mark the Route If Necessary" in chapter 6.) Once you know that you have an identifiable object or marker along your bearing line, you can walk around

If your route is blocked by an obstruction like a lake, try to find a large, easily visible object on your bearing line before you start traveling past the obstruction.

the obstruction using whatever route is easiest. Once past the obstruction, *take a back bearing on your starting point.* If this does not match the bearing of your intended direction of travel, then continue around the obstruction until your back bearing on the starting point *does* match your intended direction of travel.

A REMINDER

Wherever possible, *navigate by using trails and natural topographic features*, while keeping track of your position on the map. Reserve the use of navigation by instrument for those situations where there is no other alternative.

If the obstruction is a cliff, hill, or some other feature that prevents you from seeing your starting point once you have passed the obstruction, then you may have to use a different technique, as shown in figure 3-13. In this case, you can travel a paced distance at 90 degrees to the original course, then go past the blockage on a bearing parallel to the original course, and finally return to the original course by another 90-degree course change paced the same distance as the earlier one but in the opposite direction. (The course change need not be 90 degrees. It could be 45 degrees or some other direction, as long as it is easily possible to return to the original direction of travel.)

ALWAYS KEEP THE RETURN ROUTE IN MIND

No party should ever wander off on what may appear to be an obvious route without taking note of the direction they are heading and planning how they will return.

Example: Suppose a party follows a trail to a camp in the forest (fig. 3-14). After eating dinner, they decide to hike off-trail to a clearly visible pass to see the view. After enjoying a memorable sunset at the pass, they turn around to return to camp. At that point it occurs to them that they cannot see their camp, do not know the direction to it, and will shortly be running out of daylight. Is this a problem? It all depends on the preparations they made on the hike to the pass.

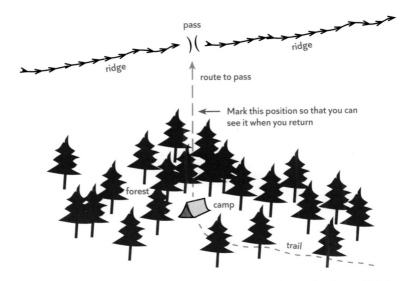

Fig. 3-14. *Example of traveling via an obvious route to a destination from which the return trip will not be obvious*

If they had merely headed up to the pass without any thought of how they would get back, they might be in trouble. If, on the other hand, they had taken a compass bearing from their camp to the pass when they started their trek, then once at the pass they could simply follow a back bearing from the pass to return to their camp in the forest. They could have also used route-marking materials to mark the spot where they emerged from the forest. (If you do this, be sure to remove the marker once you no longer need it. Good wilderness travelers practice leave-no-trace principles: take only pictures, leave only footprints.) These simple measures could turn a potentially serious problem into a routine after-dinner stroll.

CHAPTER SUMMARY

In this chapter you learned about orientation and navigation by following trails and natural topographic features as well as by using a map and compass. You also learned about the usefulness of the intentional offset and other techniques. Finally, you now understand the importance of maintaining map awareness of where you are at all times.

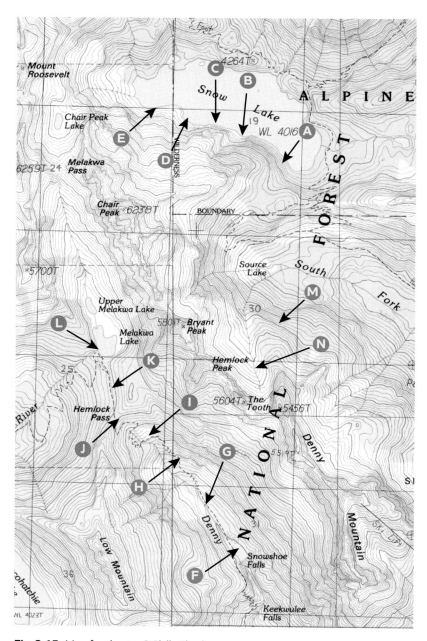

Fig. 3-15. *Map for chapter 3 Skills Check*

1. From Source Lake, you see an imposing-looking peak and wish to identify it. You measure its bearing with your compass and obtain 290°. What is the name and altitude of the peak?

2. You are at Source Lake and wish to identify which of the many peaks around you is The Tooth. What bearing would you set on your compass in order to make it point toward The Tooth?

3. You are somewhere on the south shore of Snow Lake but don't know exactly where. You take a bearing on Bryant Peak and get 194°. What letter on the map identifies your position?

4. You are hiking along the Denny Creek Trail north of Snowshoe Falls when you spot The Tooth. You take a bearing on it and get 42°. What letter on the map identifies your position?

5. What bearing would you follow to get from Hemlock Peak to the Denny Creek Trail using the shortest straight-line distance?

6. You are lost, but you can see and identify some mountain peaks near you. You take a bearing on Chair Peak and get 16°. You can also see Bryant Peak, and its bearing is 104°. Where are you?

7. You are somewhere on this map. You wish to go to Hemlock Pass. You take a bearing on Bryant Peak and get 21°. You can also see Denny Mountain, and its bearing is 63°. What bearing should you follow to get to Hemlock Pass?

8. What is the bearing of the slope in degrees, looking downhill from point M?

   a. 212°   b. 120°   c. 300°   d. 32°

9. From point N you take a bearing on the slope looking downhill and get 345°. What is the bearing of the slope pointing uphill from that point?

10. What is the elevation loss from the summit of Low Mountain to the Denny Creek trail, if following the stream gully to the northeast? Would this be the easiest route to get to the trail? Is so, why? If not, what route would you suggest?

CHECK YOUR ANSWERS. How did you do? If you got all the questions right, then proceed with confidence to the next chapter! If you got some wrong or could not answer some, reread the pertinent sections of this chapter before proceeding on to the next.

CHAPTER 4

THE ALTIMETER

CHAPTER OBJECTIVES

- Explain the types and general features of altimeters.
- Describe effects of barometric pressure and temperature on altimeter readings.
- Explain the difference between altimeter accuracy and precision.
- Explain the use of altimeters in orientation and navigation.
- Show how altimeters can aid in your decision-making.
- Explain how altimeters can help to predict the weather.

An altimeter, like a compass, provides one simple piece of crucial information: **elevation**. Wilderness travelers can keep track of their progress, verify their location, and find their way to critical junctions on the route by monitoring their elevation and checking it against their topographic map. In mountainous terrain, the altimeter can be a great help in orientation, navigation, and routefinding.

Types of Altimeters

There are two basic operating types of altimeters: those that detect changes in barometric pressure, and those that display elevation based on signals from GPS satellites (see chapter 5). A pressure-based altimeter is basically a modified barometer. Pressure-based altimeters and barometers both measure air pressure (the weight of air). A **barometer** displays air pressure on a scale calibrated in inches of mercury, millibars, kilopascals, or other units of pressure. A **pressure-based altimeter** also measures air pressure, but its display is calibrated in feet or meters above sea level. This is possible because air pressure changes at a known, predictable rate

Fig. 4-1. *Digital wristwatch altimeter and analog altimeter*

with changing altitude. The higher the altitude, the lower the air pressure. Altimeters that receive signals from GPS satellites can also display altitude as long as they have a reasonably good view of the sky.

> **Tip:** When starting a technical rock-climbing pitch, remove your wristwatch altimeter (or any other jewelry, including rings or bracelets, for that matter) and attach it to your shoulder strap, or put it into your pack or pocket, to keep it from getting damaged on the rock or stuck in a crack.

The most popular physical form of wilderness altimeter is the digital wristwatch type (fig. 4-1). A digital altimeter has several advantages over the analog type. Some digital altimeters display additional information, such as heart rate, and some have compasses and thermometers. These include altimeter-barometer-compass (ABC) digital watches. Some units add GPS capability. Wristwatch altimeters are often preferred because they combine multiple functions into one piece of equipment. They also allow for instant access and therefore will be consulted more frequently than an altimeter kept in a pocket or pack. Digital altimeters are also generally more precise than analog types.

A disadvantage of a digital altimeter is that it requires a battery. However, battery life for altimeters is generally measured in months or years, depending on usage, and the battery is usually rechargeable, so this is not a serious concern. Additionally, the liquid crystal display (LCD) can go blank at subfreezing temperatures, making it essential you keep the instrument relatively warm. This is usually not a problem as long as the altimeter is worn on the wrist, under clothing. If it gets cold enough for the LCD to go blank, the altimeter still retains all of its data and will display the data properly once it warms up enough for the display to work.

The **analog altimeter** has the advantage of being a cheaper and simpler instrument. It requires no battery and continues to display the elevation even at temperatures well below 0°F (−18°C). Analog altimeters have the disadvantage of having lower precision than digital altimeters, sometimes with a 100-foot interval between altitude scale markings. To read an analog altimeter, hold it level in the palm of your hand. Look directly down on the needle, with your eyes at least a foot (30 centimeters) above it, to reduce errors due to parallax (viewing angle). Tap it lightly several times to overcome any friction in the mechanism.

Smartphones can display altitude data if a GPS or altimeter app is installed. Dedicated GPS devices also display altitude. Either can provide your elevation, though both require some time (up to several minutes) after you turn them on to acquire satellites and display data, and battery life can be a serious limitation on long-term use. This will be discussed in more detail in chapter 5.

A very wide range of altimeters is available, from simple analog devices costing under $100, to units with a huge array of sophisticated features costing up to $1000 or more. See table 4-1 for summaries of altimeter types and their characteristics.

Additional details of these and other such devices are available on the manufacturers' websites. They can be purchased at most outdoor

Table 4-1. COMPARISON OF DIFFERENT TYPES OF ALTIMETERS			
Altimeter type	Cost (US$)	Advantages	Disadvantages
Digital wristwatch or smartwatch	$$$–$$$$$	Convenient to carry; elevation instantly displayed at a glance on the user's wrist; can synch with a smartphone. Inexpensive units are acceptable for many activities. Batteries have a long life and are rechargeable.	Pressure-sensing types must be calibrated at a known altitude at the start of your trip. LCD displays can go blank at subfreezing temperatures (usually not a problem if worn under clothing).
Analog altimeter	$$–$$$$	Does not need batteries; operates in subfreezing temperatures. Inexpensive units are acceptable for many activities.	The displayed precision is never as good as with digital devices. Some units' smallest displayed interval is 100 feet. They cannot be worn as a watch on your wrist.
Smartphone GPS app	$	Same advantages as smartwatch except for instant display. The large display can show position on downloaded topographic maps. GPS-derived elevation is not subject to weather-sensitive barometric-pressure changes as pressure-sensing units are.	Same disadvantages as digital wristwatches; requires some time to acquire satellites, so altitude display is not as instantly available as with wristwatch units; not as easily accessible as those worn on a wrist.
Dedicated GPS device	$$$–$$$$$	Replaceable AA batteries used in most dedicated GPS devices, though some have rechargeable batteries. They can be used as a backup altimeter or GPS device if your phone battery is exhausted.	Needs time to acquire satellites before altitude is displayed, so altitude display is not as instantly available as with other units. The LCD screen can go blank at subfreezing temperatures.

$: $1–49, $$: $50–75, $$$: $75–99, $$$$: $100–499, $$$$$: $> $500

recreation stores and websites. If you intend to use the device in casual hiking, the most appropriate unit might be a simple, inexpensive digital wristwatch altimeter that displays the time and the altitude to the nearest five meters or less, and little else. Consider the type of terrain in which you intend to travel. If you travel off-trail in mountainous terrain, an altimeter is a nearly indispensable aid. If you never intend to leave the flatlands, where there are no appreciable elevation changes, an altimeter might be a waste of money for you.

Precision and Accuracy

A typical high-quality digital altimeter may have a resolution, or **precision** (smallest marked division), of 1 meter (about 3 feet). This does not mean that it will always have high **accuracy** (closeness to the truth). Changes in weather could easily throw a pressure-based altimeter reading off by hundreds of feet or meters, even if it is highly precise. GPS-based units can also have errors, particularly if the view of the sky is partially blocked by forests or deep canyons; keep this in mind when evaluating altimeters. Some of the least-expensive wristwatch altimeters have a resolution of 5 meters (16 feet) but may be perfectly acceptable for your activities, even though some of your companions may boast that their altimeters are better than yours because they have a 1-meter resolution. Both will be affected by these inaccuracies, which can introduce errors far exceeding their degree of precision.

EFFECTS OF BAROMETRIC PRESSURE ON ALTIMETERS

The accuracy of a pressure-based altimeter depends on the weather, because a change in the weather is usually accompanied by a change in barometric (air) pressure, which causes an error in the altimeter's reading. A change in barometric pressure of 1 inch of mercury corresponds to a change in altitude of roughly 1000 feet. (A pressure change of 10 millibars corresponds to about 100 meters of elevation change.)

Example: While you are in camp overnight, the air pressure increases by 0.2 inches of mercury, or 7 millibars (e.g., from 30.0 to 30.2 inches, or from 1016 to 1023 millibars). Therefore, your pressure-based altimeter will show a reading roughly 200 feet (60 meters) less than it did when you arrived at the campsite, even though you have remained in the same place. If you had gone out on a hike during that same day, your elevation readings by the end of the day would likewise have been about 200 feet (60 meters) too low. During periods of unstable weather, the elevation indicated on your altimeter may change by as much as 500 feet (150 meters) in one day even though your actual elevation has remained the same. Even during apparently stable conditions, an indicated change in elevation of 100 feet (30 meters) per day is not uncommon.

EFFECTS OF TEMPERATURE ON ALTIMETERS

The altimeter pressure sensor expands and contracts due to variations in temperature, causing changes in the indicated elevation. **Temperature-compensated altimeters** adjust for this effect *when there is no actual change in elevation*. When you are gaining or losing elevation, however, this compensation is often not enough, resulting in errors even in temperature-compensated altimeters.

Cautions When Using an Altimeter

Because of the strong influence of temperature and barometric pressure on a pressure-based altimeter's accuracy, *you cannot trust the instrument until you first set it at a known elevation*, such as a trailhead. It is also helpful to *check its reading whenever you reach other points of known elevation* shown on a map, so you can reset it if necessary, or at least be aware of the error. GPS-based altimeters should also be occasionally checked against map elevations, particularly under conditions of dense forest canopy or in deep canyons. Get to know your altimeter, use it often, check it at every opportunity, and note differences between its reading and that shown on your map. You will soon learn just what level of accuracy to expect, and your altimeter will become a dependable aid when roving the wilds.

COPING WITH TEMPERATURE CHANGES

To minimize the effects of temperature changes, try to keep the altimeter's temperature as constant as possible. Body heat will usually accomplish this with a wristwatch altimeter, particularly if it is worn under a parka when the outside temperature is low. With an analog altimeter, you can keep its temperature relatively constant by carrying it in your pocket rather than in your pack. Furthermore, you are more likely to use the altimeter when it is readily accessible, such as in your pocket, than if you have to take your pack off to access it.

Using an Altimeter in Wilderness Travel

It's nice to know your elevation, but how is this information actually useful? Using an altimeter can be a big help to you in orientation, navigation, decision-making, and weather prediction.

ORIENTATION

An altimeter can help you determine exactly where you are. If you are climbing a ridge, following a stream up a gully, or hiking up a trail shown on the map, but you do not know exactly where you are along the ridge, stream, or trail, check the altimeter for the elevation. Where the ridge, stream, or trail reaches that contour line on the map is your likely location. Remember that the goal of orientation is point position: determining your exact position. The feature you are following gives you line position, but you need one more piece of information to get point position. An altimeter reading can give you that knowledge.

NAVIGATION

Navigation becomes easier with an altimeter. For example, if you top a convenient couloir and gain the ridge you want to ascend, make a note of the elevation of that point in a notebook or on your map. On your return, descend the ridge to that same elevation—as indicated on your altimeter—and you should easily find the couloir again, even if clouds have come in and obscured all visibility.

Hiking and climbing guidebooks sometimes specify a change of direction or the location of a camp or other site at a particular elevation. If you are on an open snowfield or a forested hillside, the altimeter can tell you when that point is reached. The route you have worked out on a topographic map also may depend on course changes at certain elevations, and again the altimeter will keep your party on target.

WISE DECISION-MAKING

The altimeter can help you to decide whether to continue a trip or turn back by letting you calculate your rate of ascent. Suppose you have been checking the time and elevation during a climb. You note that the party gained 500 feet (150 meters) in the past hour. You know that the destination is at an elevation of 8400 feet (2560 meters), and an altimeter reading shows you are now at 6400 feet (1950 meters), so you still need to gain 2000 feet (about 600 meters). You can therefore predict that it will take roughly four more hours to reach your destination. Take that information, courtesy of the altimeter, combine it with a look at the weather, the time of the day, and the condition of team members, and you have the data on which to base a sound decision as to whether to proceed with the trip or turn back.

PREDICTING THE WEATHER

A pressure-based altimeter can help in predicting the weather, since barometric pressure decreases with increasing altitude. An altimeter reading that shows an increase in elevation when no actual elevation change has taken place (e.g., at camp overnight) means a falling barometer, which often predicts deteriorating weather. An altimeter reading that shows a decrease in elevation, on the other hand, means increasing barometric pressure and possibly improving weather. This is an oversimplification, of course. Weather forecasting is complicated by the wind, local weather peculiarities, and the rate of barometric pressure change, so don't get overly confident in predicting weather based on altimeter/barometer readings alone. Make frequent observations of altimeter readings and weather patterns on your trips—and even while at home—if you want to discern the relationship between weather and altimeter readings in your particular geographic area.

Some digital wristwatch altimeters have the option to display barometric pressure instead of altitude. But keep in mind that *changes in barometric pressure are useful in assessing the weather only when the readings are taken at a constant elevation* (e.g., in camp). Using the altimeter as a barometer while you are ascending or descending will give readings that are influenced not only by changes in barometric pressure but also by changes in your elevation as you travel. Your conclusions about barometric pressure trends may be erroneous under such circumstances.

USE OF BEARING OF THE SLOPE WITH AN ALTIMETER

The **bearing of the slope** (described in chapter 3) becomes a powerful tool when combined with altimeter use. Sometimes, when on a feature-less snow slope, in a dense forest, or in foggy conditions, it is impossible to take bearings on visible landmarks, and there are no identifiable topographic features for you to compare to your map. Under these and similar conditions, knowing your altitude plus the bearing of the slope can often provide enough information to enable you to determine your position with a high degree of certainty. For example, in the situation illustrated in figure 1-10, if you knew your elevation was 5400 feet from an altimeter, you would know that you are somewhere on or near the contour line at that elevation. If you know the slope falls off to the east, point H is the only place on that contour line where this is true, so that is your location.

ALTITUDE FUNCTION IN GPS DEVICES

Smartphones with GPS apps and dedicated GPS devices display both altitude and position, so having one of these devices can eliminate the need for an altimeter. But there are disadvantages to relying on them for

A pressure-based altimeter can help to predict and prepare for changes in weather.

altitude information. First, the batteries in digital wristwatch altimeters have lifetimes usually measured in months or years, and analog altimeters do not depend on batteries at all, whereas those in dedicated GPS devices and in smartphones with GPS apps are limited to hours or days, depending on usage. Second, though GPS-indicated altitude has a resolution of about one yard or one meter, these devices' altitude accuracy is not as good as their ground-position accuracy, and they can have errors of 100 feet (about 30 meters) or even more when sky visibility is limited, such as in thick forests or deep canyons. Also, digital and analog altimeters continuously display altitude, always available at a glance, whereas GPS devices may need several minutes to acquire a valid position after being powered up. For these reasons, many serious mountain travelers choose to wear a digital wristwatch altimeter or carry an analog altimeter, even if they are also carrying a GPS device.

CHAPTER SUMMARY

This chapter covered different types and characteristics of altimeters, what they do and how they work, and the distinction between resolution (precision) and accuracy. You now know how to select an altimeter and how to use it for orientation, navigation, decision-making, and weather prediction.

SKILLS CHECK

See the appendix for answers.

1. **List three advantages of a digital wristwatch altimeter over an analog altimeter.**

2. **List three advantages of an analog altimeter over a digital altimeter.**

3. **Precision means:**

   a. closeness to the true value
   b. quality of construction
   c. smallest indicated interval
   d. relative cost

4. **Accuracy means:**

   a. closeness to the true value
   b. quality of construction
   c. smallest indicated interval
   d. relative cost

5. **When altitude increases, barometric pressure:**

   a. increases
   b. decreases
   c. remains the same
   d. becomes unstable

6. **When starting an outdoor adventure, what must you always do to a pressure-based altimeter?**

7. **What advantage does a wristwatch altimeter have over a GPS device or app that also indicates elevation?**

   a. better accuracy   b. better precision   c. instant access   d. none

8. **What advantage does a GPS device or phone GPS app that also indicates elevation have over a pressure-sensing wristwatch altimeter?**

   a. better accuracy
   b. better precision
   c. instant access
   d. no need to set its altitude at a known position

9. **If a pressure-based altimeter shows a decrease in elevation at camp overnight while you have stayed in the same place, what would you expect in the next day's weather?**

   a. no change
   b. improving conditions
   c. deteriorating conditions
   d. a decrease in temperature
   e. an increase in temperature

10. **Does a temperature-compensated altimeter always compensate for temperature? Why or why not?**

CHECK YOUR ANSWERS. How did you do? If you got all the questions right, then proceed with confidence to the next chapter! If you got some wrong or could not answer some, reread the pertinent sections of this chapter before proceeding on to the next.

CHAPTER 5

SATELLITE NAVIGATION & COMMUNICATION

- Learn about the Global Positioning System (GPS).
- Understand how to prepare for a trip using GPS.
- Learn how to use GPS efficiently on a trip.
- Understand the limitations of the GPS.
- Learn about satellite communication devices

The United States' Department of Defense has placed a system of GPS satellites in orbit around the Earth. Other countries have created their own systems, including Russia's GLONASS, the European Union's Galileo, and similar systems installed by China, India, and Japan. GPS devices receive signals from these satellites and process them to determine the user's geographic position and altitude to as close as about 10 feet (3 meters) under ideal sky conditions. The device can also tell you the distance and direction from your position to any other position. In other words, the system can provide you with precise orientation and navigation in the absence of any visible landmarks. This development has revolutionized navigation on the ground, in the air, and on the water.

Selecting a GPS Device

In this book, the general term "GPS device" refers to any electronic device capable of receiving and processing GPS signals and displaying the user's geographic position and altitude. This includes phones with GPS apps installed on them (even out of the limited range of cell phone antennas), watches with GPS capability, dedicated GPS devices such as those made by Garmin, and satellite-based communication devices. A comparison of these devices is shown in table 5-1.

Getting Started with GPS

When using a GPS device, avoid the temptation to rush out into the wilderness, get lost, and trust that this marvelous electronic instrument will magically get you home again. Instead, carefully read the device's instruction manual and get acquainted and proficient with its use at home. (This chapter is intended only as a supplement to the instruction manual that comes with your GPS device or app.)

Select which units to use (miles or kilometers, feet or meters, magnetic or true bearings, etc.) and—very important—select the device's datum to agree with the datum shown on the paper topographic map of the area that you are also carrying. For dedicated GPS devices, these options are generally accessible using the device's settings screen. Watches and phones with GPS apps automatically set their datum (WGS 84 is the default datum) to match the datum of their displayed map. If you are using the compass methods described in chapter 2, be sure to use true bearings (usually the default north reference setting) rather than magnetic bearings. Try out the device around your home, in city parks, and on easy trail hikes before taking it into the wilderness.

The most important rule for using any GPS device is to avoid becoming totally dependent on it. It is best to consider the GPS device to be an extra navigational tool—a useful addition to a paper map and a magnetic baseplate compass—rather than as a replacement for them. If conditions warrant, carry route-marking materials such as wands regardless of whether you have a GPS device. *Never rely solely on any GPS device for navigation.*

Using a Dedicated GPS Device in Wilderness Navigation

To minimize battery usage, you can use your GPS device along with a map and compass in order to ensure that you can get back to your starting point. For example, at the road end, trailhead, campsite, or wherever you start your trip, turn the device on to establish your GPS position. Compare the displayed coordinates to your map to ensure that they make sense. (Under rare conditions, erroneous positions can be displayed.) If the position looks valid, save this position as a **waypoint**; give it a unique name (e.g., "CAR" or "CAMP") if desired. Then turn off the device to save battery power, and pack it away carefully to protect it from harm while you are traveling. Along the route, you may encounter crucial locations, such as important

Table 5-1. COMPARISON OF VARIOUS TYPES OF GPS DEVICES			
Device type	**Cost (US$)**	**Advantages**	**Disadvantages**
Smartphones with GPS apps installed	$$$– $$$$$	Most users already have such phones. GPS apps can be added to phones for minimal cost; some are free. They have a familiar user interface and large screen.	Non-user-replaceable batteries last a few days; it is difficult to see the screen in bright conditions, and LCD displays can go blank at subfreezing temperatures.
GPS watches	$$$– $$$$$	Position is displayed in latitude/longitude or UTM, and they are easily accessible. ABC units have an altimeter, barometer, and compass.	Maps are shown only on the most expensive units. Batteries usually must be recharged with proprietary cables or magnetically.
Dedicated GPS devices	$$$$– $$$$$ (Map resolution increases with more expensive units.)	User-replaceable AA batteries are used in most dedicated GPS devices. Rugged construction.	LCD displays can go blank at subfreezing temperatures. The most expensive units have topographic maps preinstalled on some models; others need to be installed using home computer or SD cards at added cost.
Satellite-based communicators (PLBs and satcoms)	$$$$– $$$$$	Personal locator beacons (PLBs) find location via GPS and can send a signal to a rescue agency. Satcoms (satellite communicators) allow one- or two-way communication.	PLBs are inexpensive to use but are for emergency rescue only. Satellite communicators require a paid subscription and may incur additional costs for messages; they can be expensive.

$: $1–49, $$: $50–75, $$$: $75–99, $$$$: $100–499, $$$$$: >$500

trail junctions, a ridge crest, or a crevasse or other hazard. At such points, turn on the device to establish additional waypoints. Again, make sure their coordinates match those on the map. Once you are at your destination or turnaround point, use the device to find the distance and compass bearing from one waypoint to another to return to the starting point. Then turn off the device and follow a trail or topography, or use your compass to travel to the next waypoint. At any point at which you turn on the device and get a position, you can ask it to "go to" any previously stored waypoint. It will then provide the distance and compass bearing to that waypoint.

Many GPS instruction manuals seem to assume that you are always traveling with the device turned on and in your hand, constantly observing its display. Doing this wastes battery power and occupies a hand that might be better used for climbing, scrambling, or holding an ice axe or trekking pole. In addition, it distracts you from observing the route, its hazards, and the scenery—and it looks really nerdy. *The most efficient way to use a GPS device is to use it only occasionally* and to travel by map, compass, and topography or trails the rest of the time.

Under some conditions it might be advantageous to leave a GPS device turned on continuously while you travel—such as when you are descending through a forest, navigating a snow slope in a whiteout, or traveling when it's late and darkness is approaching. Under such conditions, every minute might count, making it impractical to stop for a few minutes every now and then to turn the device on and wait for it to reacquire your position (which might require a minute or two, or even more in some situations).

> **Tip:** If you want to leave the device turned on so that you can refer to it continuously, securely attach it to a pack strap or some other easily accessible place so your hands are free while you travel. Then you can look at it any time you want while using your hands for other purposes.

If you decide to leave your GPS device on as you travel toward your destination, it can record your route as a track. Then on your return trip, you can use its backtrack mode to retrace your steps very closely. This feature can only be used if you leave it on the entire time both en route to your destination and on the return trip. This method will exhaust batteries much more quickly than occasional use, so we suggest that you only use this technique sparingly.

Start each wilderness trip with a fresh set of batteries and spares (for a dedicated GPS device), or with a fully charged phone and possibly a fully charged battery pack (for a phone with a GPS app).

GPS devices have some obvious advantages over magnetic compasses. A compass can help you find your position only if you can see landmarks and can take bearings on them. The GPS, on the other hand, can provide your position without any visible landmarks (under acceptable conditions). This can be particularly helpful in fog or a whiteout or in featureless terrain.

In chapter 3 we described various strategies to use to follow a compass bearing toward your objective, such as using intermediate objectives, aiming off, and detouring around an obstruction. When using a compass, such techniques are essential in order to stay on your correct course. With GPS, however, navigation becomes easier. If you are trying to follow a given bearing to your destination and the route is blocked, you can simply travel around the blockage by the easiest route without considering how far off route you get or in what direction. Once past the obstruction, you can again turn on your GPS device and obtain a new position, and it will provide the new bearing to your objective. Then you can set that new bearing on your compass and follow it.

> **Tip:** When planning a wilderness trip, find the coordinates of critical sites (e.g., the starting point, critical junctions and landmarks, the destination) on the map and enter them into your GPS device as waypoints. This is easiest to do at home before your trip.

Interfacing a GPS Device with a Home Computer

Many dedicated GPS devices and GPS watches can be *paired* with a home desktop or laptop computer to enhance their functionality. This allows the user to view topographic maps on a large-screen monitor, establish and manage waypoints, prepare complex route plans, and transfer them to the GPS device. After a wilderness adventure, the user can download the trip track and waypoints taken on the trip onto their computer for posttrip analysis and reporting and for future reference and sharing with others.

Limitations of GPS Devices

A GPS device is not a substitute for a map and compass or the ability to use them. Most GPS devices can tell you the straight-line route from one point to another, but they have no way of knowing if there is a river, a lake, or a cliff along this route. For this reason, you still must have a topographic map with you, even if you also have a GPS device. Many dedicated GPS devices, and all phones with GPS apps, can display topographic maps and can show your position directly on the screen. While this is a very useful feature, *it does not replace the need for conventional paper maps* because you still need to be able to view the big picture of the route and avoid total dependence on the GPS device. Furthermore, using electronic maps requires a great deal of panning and zooming in and out, which can be tedious and time- and power-consuming. It is easier and quicker to simply glance at a paper topographic map.

Some GPS devices contain built-in electronic compasses. Using such an instrument might eliminate the need to use your baseplate compass. You could then conceivably do all your navigating using only your GPS device. Even then, however, *you still need to carry a magnetic compass*, in case the GPS device's compass loses its calibration (which can happen when the batteries are replaced), or if the device is dropped or bumped, exhausts its batteries, gets wet, or otherwise fails to work properly. Your compass will never become inoperative due to dead batteries.

Most GPS devices will not work at temperatures much below freezing, and battery life is limited to fifteen to thirty hours, depending on the model and the type of batteries used.

GPS devices must track signals from at least four satellites in order to provide trustworthy position information. If the satellite signals are blocked by heavy forest cover, cliffs, or canyons, this may not be possible. When a GPS device is not able to receive signals from four satellites, it sacrifices altitude information in favor of horizontal position. Some devices indicate that this is happening by displaying a "2D" message, signaling that it is operating in a two-dimensional mode. Some receivers merely display a "frozen" altitude display if this occurs. In either case, *always note whether you are getting a two-dimensional position.* If so, then be aware of the fact that the GPS device's horizontal position may be significantly in error as well, particularly if you are at a high altitude. Under such less-than-ideal conditions, horizontal position errors of 1000 feet (hundreds of meters) or more are possible.

Because of the slight possibility that a GPS device might have a position error, it is wise to exercise caution before using or saving a waypoint. For example, suppose you are in a parking lot at a trailhead and you acquire a GPS position. This will be an important waypoint, since you will certainly want to get back to your vehicle at the end of your trek. Instead of just mindlessly saving this position, you should *first observe the coordinates indicated on the screen* of the device and *compare them to your map.* These coordinates should indicate a position very close to your known location. Also, observe the elevation indicated on the GPS device's screen, and compare it with that shown on your map or altimeter. Again, they should agree closely. Any significant difference between either your known position or altitude and that shown on the GPS device should alert you to the possibility that you might have an erroneous GPS position, perhaps due to signal reflections off cliffs, cars, or other structures, or perhaps due to some atmospheric disturbance. In this case, wait a few minutes or walk a short distance and try again. Do not save any important waypoint until you have verified that it is in reasonable agreement with your position as shown on the map.

Coping with the Limitations of GPS Devices

A variety of conditions can prevent a GPS device from giving you the information you need for navigation in the wilderness: deep canyons or heavy forest cover that prevent acquisition of enough satellite signals to obtain a position; outside temperatures below the minimum required for the device's LCD display; large inaccuracies caused by multipath signals due to reflections of satellite signals; depletion of battery life; loss of or damage to the device; and electronic failure. These conditions are generally rare and in many cases preventable. Still, such conditions can and do occur. Although it is impossible to prevent all problems and inaccuracies, with a little forethought and planning it should be possible to get to your objective and back home safely even without a functioning GPS device.

COLD-TEMPERATURE OPERATION

Every GPS device has a lower-temperature operating limit, below which it will not display any data due to inherent characteristics of its display. Various devices have different temperature requirements, but generally this lower limit is somewhere between −5°F and +14°F (−20°C and −10°C), depending on the particular unit. You can usually find this information in the specifications section of the user manual. If you contemplate using the unit in such conditions, you should *test its cold-temperature operation at or near your home in cold conditions* (e.g., in your refrigerator's freezer) before you trust it to operate in a cold climate. If you need it to operate at a temperature lower than its lower limit, carry it close to your body in a pocket or other location under several layers of clothing. Most GPS devices are not permanently damaged due to exposure to cold temperatures, and many still operate and can track your position under such conditions but simply cannot display your position. They usually return to normal operation after they warm up. Phones with GPS apps are generally somewhat more sensitive to temperature extremes than dedicated devices. Also, the touchscreen displays of smartphones do not always respond to gloved fingers. Dedicated devices generally have mechanical buttons instead of touchscreens, so they do not have that problem. If you plan on using a touchscreen device for GPS, then wear touchscreen-compatible gloves. These have special fingertips with conductive material that allow for the touchscreen to respond to input. Phones may also exhibit problems if exposed to temperatures greater than about 95°F (35°C). Under these conditions, the device may display a warning sign or may shut down.

MAXIMIZING BATTERY LIFE

Many GPS users—of both dedicated and smartphone devices—complain that their devices exhaust their batteries at a faster rate than expected. There are a few things that you can do to increase battery life. In dedicated GPS devices with user-replaceable batteries, you can *use longer-lasting lithium batteries* rather than standard alkaline batteries. Lithium cells cost more but may save you money in the long run since they last longer. Furthermore, they work more reliably at cold temperatures and weigh less.

If you *operate your GPS device at a moderate temperature*, its batteries will last longer. You should keep the device and any spare batteries out of direct sunlight, and inside your jacket on cold days.

Turn your device off when navigation is easy or straightforward, such as while walking along a good, well-maintained trail, as well as when you are in heavy forest cover or in a canyon where the unit will waste power trying to search for signals that it cannot receive.

Additional battery-saving techniques for GPS devices include reducing backlight brightness and the display timeout period for the screen's light dimmer. Most devices allow you to set the brightness and timeout time to lower values than the default conditions. Also, *disable power drainers* such as the compass and barometer if they are not being used. If the device has accuracy-enhancing features like WAAS (Wide Area Augmentation System) or SBAS (Space [or Satellite] Based Augmentation System), you should be able to turn them off to prevent the unit from wasting power when trying to access satellites it cannot find.

CONVENTIONAL MAP-AND-COMPASS NAVIGATION

Of course, the most important method of coping with any GPS problem is your ability to fall back on conventional map-and-compass navigational techniques. Again, do not become totally dependent on your GPS device. *Always carry a baseplate compass and a paper topographic map* of the area in which you are traveling, even if the device has an electronic compass and/or a digital map of the area. You should never allow yourself to get into a situation where the failure of an electronic device will jeopardize your safety or your ability to get back home.

Using the GPS Function in Smartphones

For many of us, smartphones have become an integral part of our modern world. This section explains how to best use these devices for navigation in the wilderness environment.

Smartphones receive signals from three sources: a Wi-Fi network, the cellular network, and GPS satellites. The ranges of these signals are several hundred feet for Wi-Fi signals and a few miles for cellular phone signals. GPS signals, however, can travel thousands of miles and are available almost anywhere on Earth. In wilderness travel you are usually traveling outside of Wi-Fi and cellular range and are using GPS signals alone.

DOWNLOADING MAPS ONTO PHONES

Most smartphones (i.e., those can access the internet) have GPS capability. They can display your position on a digital map (see fig. 5-1). These topographic maps are not transmitted to your device through the GPS satellite signal. Instead, they must be downloaded through a Wi-Fi connection, if one is available, or through the slower, cellular network, neither of which is usually available in the wilderness. If you have not downloaded

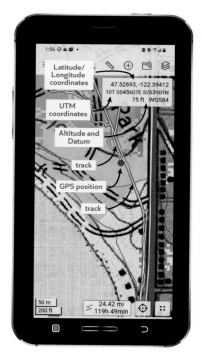

Fig. 5-1. Example screen display of a smartphone GPS app showing position, altitude, and tracks

Fig. 5-2. How position is shown on a smartphone when out of cellular range with no map downloaded

the maps for the area in which you will be traveling, and you are out of Wi-Fi and cell tower range, your smartphone may be able to display your position from the GPS signals, but only as a dot on a grid or a blank screen (see fig. 5-2). Therefore, load maps of your entire route, plus a large amount of the surrounding area, onto your smartphone at home before embarking on your adventure in the wilderness.

If you have not previously downloaded a map of the area and just get a dot on a grid, or if your smartphone displays a message like "outside of the cellular network" or "search results not available," you should still be able to find your location by getting the device to display the latitude/longitude or UTM coordinates (at the top of fig. 5-2) even if the map is not displayed. Then you can find your position on the paper map that you will also be carrying. Most topographic maps have UTM marks around the periphery of the map and often have grid lines that are far more useful than latitude and longitude (see chapter 7 for details regarding how to use the latitude/longitude and UTM systems). Always remember to examine these coordinates carefully and make sure that they make sense to you, and that they are not merely the last recorded coordinates (a common default condition of smartphones as well as dedicated GPS devices when the device cannot obtain a current satellite-position fix).

If you have wandered off the area you prepared for and have neither a paper map nor a cached smartphone map, you can take and save a series of waypoints or record a track while en route to your destination, then follow a track back, following these waypoints.

TESTING YOUR APP

To test your smartphone's GPS function, install one of the many GPS apps, such as Green Trails Maps, CalTopo, or Gaia GPS. Then go into your device's settings screen with GPS enabled (i.e., enable the location function), and simulate the wilderness-environment signal reception by turning off your Wi-Fi and cellular network access by switching to airplane mode. This leaves only the GPS signals receivable. It may take a few minutes to acquire satellites and display your position. Does it give a location that makes sense to you? Does it give a location at all? If so, make note of the displayed coordinates or take a screenshot. To ensure a good position, be sure to observe the displayed position for a few minutes. Its accuracy may improve as more satellites are acquired.

Next, take a short walk, drive, or bike ride to a familiar location. Leave it in airplane mode, with the Wi-Fi and cellular network off while doing so. Once you are some distance from where you first obtained a GPS signal, enable your GPS app and observe the coordinates once again. Compare the new coordinates with those you recorded or with the saved screenshot previously taken. Are they different? Do the new coordinates match your known position? Often, a GPS device—even a smart device—will display the last known position if a current position cannot be determined. This is why it is so important to *compare the position that the device indicates with your known position*. Bad information is worse than no information at all. If the new position agrees with your current position, then you have data that you can work with. Experiment with free apps and read reviews of paid apps to see if a particular app is worth the money for your particular needs.

If you leave the GPS function on while you travel from one place to another, you can often create a "track" showing your path on the screen. On your return trip, you can then follow this track back to your starting point.

DIGITAL MAPS

The key to successful navigation with a smartphone is downloading the most detailed maps of the area in which you will be traveling well before your journey begins. Be sure to do this in an area with a strong Wi-Fi signal, since attempting to download detailed maps while driving to remote trailheads can be slow and frustrating—if it's possible at all. Once the maps are installed, make sure the phone is fully charged before starting your trip.

BATTERY LIFE

Some of the suggestions listed in the previous section, "Maximizing Battery Life," in the general discussion of GPS devices (e.g., turn the device off when not needed or in heavy forest; disable unused functions) also apply to smartphones with GPS apps. Some additional tips for extending your smartphone's battery life include turning off power-hungry apps.

Fig. 5-3. *An external battery pack can recharge your smartphone.*

To further save battery power, *disable unused apps' "push" notifications.* This will prevent the device from waking up if that particular app is activated when you are within cell tower range by an incoming message, social media update, stock report, or traffic or news update. *Putting your phone into airplane mode will also prevent it from running unwanted apps in the background,* while still allowing GPS and camera use. (The battery life of GPS watches with fitness apps such as heart rate monitors and step counters can also be extended by disabling these apps when not needed.)

You can also *turn down the brightness of the screen and decrease the amount of time before your device enters sleep mode.* The display consumes much energy, and even a slight dimming will correlate to increased battery life. (That said, on a bright day above the tree line, the dimmed display is harder to read.) Experiment with different settings for screen brightness to see just how bright the screen really needs to be in order to be usefully visible outdoors.

The most effective way to extend battery life, of course, is to *turn off your device completely.* Turn it on only at key locations, obtain a good position that agrees with your known position, save the waypoint, and turn it off. In this way the device is only used for necessary navigation.

Table 5-2. COMPARISON OF SATELLITE COMMUNICATION DEVICES			
Device	**Satellite products**	**Functionality**	**Pros and cons**
Personal Locator Beacons (PLB)	Dedicated satellite international search and rescue system (EPIRBs and ACR ResQLink)	Obtains location from GPS and then sends it to emergency responders via government-managed satellites; for emergency use only.	Registration and/or subscription may be required.
Smartphones	Commercial satellite systems	One-way or two-way texting depending on device used; Android and Apple both have some limited capability.	Emerging technology; costs and dependability are highly variable.
Satellite communicators/ messenger device (satcom)	Commercial systems: SPOT Satellite GPS Messenger, Garmin InReach, ZOLEO	Sends location to emergency responders via private companies; can also transmit location to friends and family. Some have additional text message options.	Some models function as full GPS devices. Most require a monthly or annual subscription. Costs vary and depend on services provided.
Satellite phones	Commercial systems by private companies	Two-way backcountry telephone; some allow SMS text messaging.	Some are GPS enabled; call time is expensive.

LIMITATIONS OF USING GPS WITH SMARTPHONES

You may be accustomed to using your phone in the city, within cell tower range, and with ample access to power, but you won't be afforded such luxuries in the wilderness, where a different mindset is required.

Supplemental power sources are available for smartphones in the backcountry, including external battery packs or power banks (see fig. 5-3) and solar chargers. Since smartphone batteries can't be replaced, you do not have the option of carrying a spare battery to replace a drained one. Depending on the projected maximum length of your wilderness adventure, it is often wise to bring a fully charged external battery pack or two. It takes about 5000 milliamp-hours (mAh) to charge a typical smartphone from fully depleted to fully charged. Some battery packs have a capacity of 10,000 mAh, so they can fully charge a phone two times during a trip. If you are considering purchasing a supplemental power supply for wilderness travel, consider price, weight, milliamp-hour capacity, durability, and cold-temperature operation, if applicable. Be realistic about how many milliamp-hours you really need. Some battery packs are specifically made for cold-weather operation.

Solar chargers can be used to charge external battery packs and some phones. However, some phones cannot be directly charged by solar panels. In either case, you can charge your external battery pack during daytime travel and then use the battery pack to charge your phone at camp overnight. Some GPS watches have built-in solar charging capability.

Personal Locator Beacons (PLBs) and Satellite Communicators

There are several different types of emergency communication devices, most of which determine your location using GPS. A summary of these is shown in table 5-2.

PLBs determine a party's coordinates using GPS and can transmit them through government-installed communications satellites to appropriate emergency responders. This communication can initiate a search-and-rescue operation, possibly saving your life. Registration is required, and there may be subscription fees. When these devices are used to initiate a search-and-rescue operation, in some locations the user may be liable for the cost of the rescue, possibly in the thousands of dollars. A PLB should therefore only be used in event of an extreme emergency.

THE IMPORTANCE OF SELF-RELIANCE

Understanding the limits of electronic communication tools is as important as understanding their usefulness: Batteries deplete. Electronics fail. Cell phone service is limited in wilderness locations. A rescue effort may not be possible due to weather or personnel conditions. No party should set out ill-prepared or inadequately equipped, nor should they attempt a route beyond their ability and assume that emergency help can be summoned.

Your phone should always be your first attempt at obtaining assistance. Any cell phone can contact emergency services (e.g., 911 within the United States and Canada) if it is within range of a cell tower. In some wilderness areas, you may be able to send a text message when voice communication is not possible. If out of range of a cell tower, phones can sometimes send text messages via special communication satellites. Technology is rapidly changing and may provide more reliable emergency texting in the future. For now, however, you should assume that your phone will not work in the wilderness. Carrying a PLB or satellite messenger can add a margin of safety by enabling you to initiate a rescue effort should anyone become injured, lost, or ill.

Current satellite messengers determine your position using GPS and then send a message using commercial satellite networks, even in the thickest of forests and deepest canyons. Some support only one-way messaging of short, preset, nonemergency text messages (e.g., "Camping here tonight") or free-form text messages. Others allow two-way texting. Satellite communicators require paid subscriptions, and the cost varies based on factors such as the number of messages transmitted. At the time of publication, some countries prohibit personal use or possession of satellite communicators, so be sure to check and abide by local regulations if you are traveling.

Satellite phones are reliable and can be used for voice communication as well as texts. They are expensive to purchase, and voice communication has a high cost per minute. These are often used by large expeditions and are therefore impractical for recreational use unless cost is not an issue.

CHAPTER SUMMARY

GPS is a marvelous technology, and using it can significantly simplify wilderness navigation. Keep in mind, however, that it is not foolproof, and that topography, forest cover, limited battery life, electronic failure, cold temperatures, and inadequate user knowledge can prevent its effective use. A GPS device cannot replace conventional map-and-compass techniques, which work at temperatures well below freezing, require no batteries, function in even the thickest of forests and deepest canyons, and are so simple that there is very little that can go wrong with them. There is a good reason why the map and compass remain the basic foundation of wilderness navigation.

SKILLS CHECK
See the appendix for answers.

1. **What type of GPS device must be set to match the datum of your map?**
   a. all types
   b. only phones with GPS apps
   c. only GPS watches
   d. only dedicated GPS devices

2. **List three advantages of a phone with a GPS app over a dedicated GPS device.**

3. **List three advantages of a dedicated GPS device over a phone with a GPS app.**

4. **List three advantages of a GPS watch over both a dedicated GPS device and a phone with a GPS app.**

5. **A smartphone can be used as a GPS device only within range of cell towers.**
   a. true
   b. false

6. **If no map has been installed on your GPS device, how can you locate your position on a paper map?**
   a. You can't.
   b. Turn the device off, then restart it.
   c. Install a map while in the wilderness.
   d. Read the UTM or latitude/longitude coordinates on the GPS device and find them on the map.

7. **List four things you can do with either a dedicated GPS device or a phone with a GPS app to increase the time until its batteries are exhausted and need replacement or recharging.**

8. **List four different devices that can be used to summon emergency assistance in the wilderness.**

9. **List two advantages of a PLB over a satellite messenger.**

10. **List three advantages of a satellite messenger over a PLB.**

CHECK YOUR ANSWERS. How did you do? If you got all the questions right, then proceed with confidence to the next chapter! If you got some wrong or could not answer some, reread the pertinent sections of this chapter before proceeding on to the next.

CHAPTER 6

LOST

CHAPTER OBJECTIVES

- Know how to avoid getting lost by identifying catch lines, handrails, and potential routefinding problems.
- Learn steps you can take before and during the trip to ensure that you stay on track and do not get lost.
- Know what to do if you ever *do* get lost.

The primary focus of this book is to provide you with the necessary skills and knowledge to avoid getting lost in the first place. Later in this chapter, you will learn what to do if you ever do get lost. But you should always know where you are if you:

- have carefully read and absorbed the preceding five chapters;
- carry a topographic map of the area and a good compass;
- have adequately practiced map reading, compass use, orientation, and navigation; and
- maintain orientation at all times, by keeping track of your position on the map throughout your trip.

If you have done these things, it is unlikely that you will ever get lost, and this entire chapter may be only of academic interest to you. Combined with the information in the first five chapters, this chapter is intended to give you additional knowledge to ensure that you never get lost in the first place.

How to Avoid Getting Lost

You can minimize your likelihood of getting lost by thoroughly planning before you ever leave home and by taking certain precautions during the trip to your destination and on the return from it.

One of the primary reasons that people get lost is that they become separated from the rest of their party. You can lessen the likelihood of this occurring by insisting that the party always stays together and by assigning a responsible, experienced, and knowledgeable person to be the rear guard, or "sweep," to prevent anyone from getting lost.

On obvious trails, allow party members to travel at their own pace, but agree ahead of time to stop and regroup at certain bridges, stream crossings, and—most importantly—trail junctions. Even then do not let the group get too spread out, and agree ahead of time on places to stop and wait for everyone to catch up. If the group includes children or inexperienced members, keep them in sight at all times.

If a party member becomes fatigued or injured or otherwise wishes to head back to the trailhead alone, then it is safer to turn the entire group around rather than risk separation. It is extremely rare that a lake, mountain, or other destination will not be there on a second (or third) attempt.

BEFORE THE TRIP

Most wilderness orientation, navigation, and routefinding are done by simply looking at your surroundings and comparing them to your map. This process is often aided by making some navigational preparations before the trip, like identifying handrails, catch lines, and possible routefinding problems.

A **handrail** is a linear feature on the map that you can follow to your objective, or it may be a feature that parallels the direction in which you are heading. The handrail should be within frequent sight or sound (e.g., a noisy babbling brook) of the route, so it can serve as an aid in navigating to your intended destination. Features that you can use as handrails during a trip include roads, trails, railroad tracks, power lines, fences, cliff bands, borders of fields and meadows, ridges, valleys, lakeshores, edges of marshes, and rivers and streams.

CATCH-LINE NAVIGATION EXAMPLE

A party once began a long scramble but had to turn around due to bad weather. They started to drive home but had a flat tire on the way. While two party members changed the tire, the other passengers noticed some delicious edible mushrooms alongside the road. A little exploration revealed that the deeper into the woods they ventured, the more numerous and luscious the mushrooms became. They told the others, and after the tire was changed, they all decided to dump their pack contents in the trunk of the car and head out into the woods to fill their packs with mushrooms.

After an hour or so, sunset approached and their packs were filled, but the party had not paid any attention to where they had been going, had taken no compass bearings, and had not followed any recognizable topographic features, since the terrain was forested, flat, and featureless. Was this a problem? Not really. They knew that the road they were traveling ran almost true north–south (fig. 6-1). They also knew that they had not crossed the road, so they had to be on the east side of the road. Some party members had their compasses in their pockets, so they could easily set their compasses on a course due west. A short ramble in the woods brought them back to the road, and they could see their car. This is a classic example of catch-line navigation.

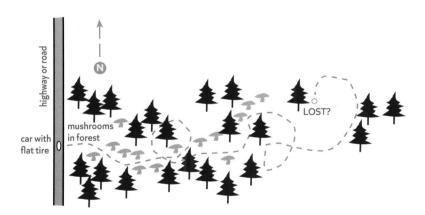

Fig. 6-1. *Example of catch-line navigation*

A **catch line** (sometimes called a "baseline") is a long, unmistakable line that always lies in the same direction from you, no matter where you are during the trip. Heading toward the catch line is a sure way to get back to your starting point if you ever get off track. It might be a handrail that you used on the way to your original objective. Pick out a catch line on the map during trip planning. It does not have to be something you can see during the trip. You just have to know that it is there, in a consistent direction from you. A catch line can be a road, an obvious trail, the shore of a large lake, a river or creek, a power line, or any other feature that is at least as long as your trip area.

If the shore of a large, distant lake always lies west of the area you will be in, you can be sure that heading west at any time will eventually get you to this identifiable landmark. Heading toward this catch line may not be the fastest way to travel back home from your destination, but it may save you from being truly lost.

Before the trip, it is wise to prepare a **route plan**: a well-thought-out description of how you will find your way to your destination and back, including handrails, catch lines, trails, topographic features you will be following, and other aspects of your proposed wilderness trek. To prepare a comprehensive route plan:

1. *Identify handrails, catch lines, and other features* that you will be following on the way to your objective. Part of this plan is to recognize potential routefinding problems. For example, if the route traverses a large, featureless area, you may need route-marking materials, particularly if the weather outlook is marginal. Be sure to carry such materials if your route plan indicates a possible need for them.

2. *Make a note of any escape routes* that can be used in case of sudden bad weather, injury, or other setbacks.

3. If off-trail travel is involved, *measure compass bearings at home before the trip* and write them down in a notebook or note them on your map. It is certainly possible to measure map bearings at any point in the trip, but it is easier and sometimes more accurate to do this at home on a desk or table, and it might save you time in an emergency.

4. *Write down and discuss your route plan* with other members of the party, so the party is not solely dependent on one person for all route decisions. You might consider requiring all party members (or at least children or inexperienced members) to carry whistles.

5. Be sure to *tell a responsible person where you are going, what route you are taking, and when you plan on returning.* This will not prevent you from getting lost, but if you do run into trouble, the authorities can be informed to look for you and where to look. *This one bit of preparation could save your life.* This could be as easy as texting a friend while you are still within cell phone range, such as "Day trip to Lk 22 with Dad and Tom. Silver Ford Fusion WA license SHWK12. Will text u when we return." It could be more elaborate, such as marking a copy of a topographic map with your planned route and emailing it to your responsible person, along with the trip schedule. It may also be a good idea to share your phone's location with one or more responsible people, if your phone has that capability. Although the technology is imperfect in the wilderness, it may give searchers a valuable clue as to your whereabouts.

> **Tip:** Be sure that you have the most recent road, trail, and avalanche conditions and a weather forecast for your trip. Check online or at the local ranger station for the latest information.

Always make sure that every member of the party carries adequate food, clothing, and other supplies (see "Survival," later in this chapter). In the event of any emergency, each person should have: enough food and clothing to survive several days, if necessary, while waiting for search-and-rescue personnel to arrive; and a map of the area and a compass, in case they become separated from the rest of the group.

Every wilderness excursion, no matter how simple, should have an agreed-upon **turnaround time**. If you have not reached your objective by this time, then you must turn around to reach the trailhead or other safe place with adequate daylight remaining. (Information on how to determine turnaround time is given in chapter 8.)

During the Trip

Get off on the right foot by making sure that everyone understands the route and the route plan:

- Gather the party around a map, and take time to discuss the route and to make contingency plans in case the party members become separated.
- Point out on the map where you are, and associate your surroundings with the piece of paper in front of you. This is a good time for everyone to make a mental note of the main features—such as forests, streams, ridges, valleys, mountain peaks, and trails—they will see during the trip.

Along the way, everyone needs to *continue associating the terrain with the map*. Ignorance of the territory is definitely not bliss for any daydreaming person who becomes separated from their party. Whenever a new landmark appears, connect it with the map. At every chance—at a pass, in a clearing, or through a break in the clouds—update your fix on the group's exact position. Keeping track of your progress on the map makes it easy to plan each succeeding leg of the trip. It may also turn you into an expert map reader because you will quickly learn what a specific valley or ridge looks like compared to its representation on the map.

Use handrails wherever possible. When the inevitable moment comes for you to leave the security of your handrail, such as a trail, make a mental note of the fact that you are leaving it, and ask yourself what you will be following instead—some topographic feature, a contour line, a compass bearing, or anything else you can count on. You should not merely press onward without a clear idea of where you are headed or how to get back.

Staying Oriented En Route

You can take several steps to stay oriented while on a wilderness trip.

LOOK AHEAD TO THE RETURN TRIP

The route often looks different on the way back. Avoid surprises and confusion by:

- glancing over your shoulder often and especially at route junctions on the way in to see what the route should look like on the return.
- recording times, elevations, landmarks, and so on. A few words, such as "7600, hit ridge," can save you a lot of grief on the return if they remind you that when the party has dropped to 7600 feet, it is time to leave the ridge and start down to your starting point.

THINK

Your brain is your most important navigational tool, a fact often overlooked amid our reliance on compasses, altimeters, and GPS devices. As the party heads toward its destination, *keep asking yourself questions*:

- How will we recognize this important spot on our return?
- What would we do if the trip leader became unconscious? (Are we all relying on one person?)
- Could I find my way back alone if I had to?
- Would we be able to find our way back in a whiteout or if snow covered our tracks?
- Should we be marking the route right now?
- How are we doing with regard to the previously agreed-upon turnaround time?

Ask these questions as you go, and act on your answers. Make decisions for you and your team before weather, route, time, and terrain make the decisions for you.

MARK THE ROUTE IF NECESSARY

There are times when it may be best to mark the route going in so you can find it again on the way out. This situation can occur when the route passes over snowfields or glaciers during changeable weather, the route goes through heavy forest, or fog threatens to hide landmarks.

On snow, climbers use thin bamboo **wands** with little flags to mark their path (see "Wands" in chapter 8).

In wooded areas, you can create temporary markers out of natural materials such as downed branches or logs. For example, at a trail junction, you can arrange branches in the shape of an arrow to point the way to the correct route, or in the shape of an X across the trail to indicate the incorrect route.

If you leave any nonnatural route markers, like wands, be sure to remove them on the return trip. Markers are litter, and good wilderness travelers never, ever litter. If there is any chance that you will not come back the same way and will not be able to remove the markers, be especially sure to use biodegradable markers, if any. For example, in the forest, plastic surveyors tape is sometimes tied to branches to show the route, but we strongly discourage its use due to its permanence, since we always endeavor to leave no trace.

If absolutely necessary, however, toilet paper could be used for a marker, because it will disintegrate during the next rainfall. Use a small streamer of toilet paper if you are assured of good weather. If not, use brightly colored crepe paper in thin rolls. It will survive the next storm, but it will most likely disintegrate during the winter.

Rock cairns (fig. 6-2) appear here and there as markers, sometimes dotting an entire route and at other times signaling the point where a

Fig. 6-2. *Rock cairns*

route changes direction. These heaps of rock are another imposition on the landscape, and they can create confusion for any traveler but the one who put them together—so do not build them. If there ever comes a time when you decide you must, then do so, but be sure to tear them down on the way out. The rule is different, however, for existing cairns. Leave them alone, on the assumption that someone else may be depending on them. *Your goal should be to leave the landscape exactly as you found it.*

KEEP TRACK

As the trip goes on, *keep yourself oriented* so that at any time you can point out your actual position to within about half a mile (roughly 1 kilometer) on the map.

Part of keeping track is having a *sense of your speed.* Given all the variables, will it take your party one hour to travel 2 miles, or will it take two hours to travel 1 mile? The answer is important if it is 3:00 p.m. and your intended campsite is still 5 miles away. After enough trips into the wilds, you will be good at estimating travel speeds. Here are some typical speeds for an average party, though there will be much variation:

- Hiking on a gentle trail with a day pack: 2 to 3 miles (3 to 5 kilometers) per hour
- Climbing up a steep trail with a full overnight pack: 1 to 2 miles (1.5 to 3 kilometers) per hour
- Traveling up a moderate slope with a day pack: 1000 feet (about 300 meters) of elevation gain per hour
- Traveling up a moderate slope with a full overnight pack: 500 feet (about 150 meters) of elevation gain per hour

In heavy brush, your rate of travel can drop to a third or even a quarter of what it would be on a good trail. Above about 10,000 feet (about 3000 meters), your rate of travel will also greatly decrease, perhaps to as little as 100 feet (30 meters) of elevation gain per hour, depending on your condition and your state of acclimatization.

On the descent if the terrain is easy, such as on a good trail or a snow-field, your rate of progress can be as much as twice the speed as on the ascent.

With a watch and a notebook (or a really good memory), you can monitor your rate of progress on any outing. Always make sure to note your starting time as well as the times you reach important streams, ridges, trail junctions, and other points along the route.

Experienced wilderness travelers regularly assess their party's progress and compare it with the route plan and the turnaround time. Estimate and reestimate when you will reach your destination and when you will return to your base camp or starting point. If it begins to look as though your party could become trapped in tricky terrain during darkness, you should discuss the situation with other members of your party; you may decide to change your plans and bivouac in a safe place or call it a day and return home.

THE RETURN TRIP

Once you are at your destination, take this golden opportunity to rest, relax, and enjoy—and to learn more about the area and about map reading by comparing the actual view with the way it looks on the map. Your destination is also the place to *lay final plans for the return*, a journey often responsible for many more routefinding problems than the way in:

- *Repeat the trailhead get-together* by discussing the route plan and emergency strategies with everyone.
- *Stress the importance of keeping the party together* on the return. Some may want to race ahead while others lag behind.

The return trip is a time to take extra care as you fight fatigue and inattention. As on the trip in, everyone needs to maintain a good sense of the route and how it relates to the map. *For a safe trip out, stay together, do not rush, and be even more careful if you are taking a different return route.*

AFTER THE TRIP

Back home, while the details are fresh in your mind, record a detailed description of the route and any problems, mistakes, or unusual features. Imagine what you would have liked to have known when you were planning the trip for the first time, so you will be ready with the right answers when another person asks about it. If a guidebook or website was confusing or wrong, take the time to propose corrections.

What If You *Do* Get Lost?

Good wilderness travelers are rarely *truly* lost—but they have also learned humility through years of experience, and they always carry enough food, clothing, and bivouac gear to get them through hours or even days of temporary confusion.

WHAT IF YOUR PARTY IS LOST?

The first rule is to *stop*. In fact, even if you *think* you may not be where you should be, *stop*!

- Resist the temptation to press onward. The moment you are ever unsure of your position, you should stop.
- Try to determine where you are. Methods of orientation are given in chapter 3.
- Keep your wits about you and do not forget what you have learned about map reading and using the compass, as explained in chapters 1 and 2.
- Study the shape of the terrain and try to associate it with your map to find out where you are.
- Remember the technique for taking the bearing of the slope as explained in chapter 3. Take a bearing on the fall line and try to associate it with your position by studying the map.

If these suggestions do not work, then try to determine the last time the group *did* know its exact location. If that spot is fairly close—within an hour or so—retrace your steps and get back on route. But if that spot is hours back, you might instead decide to head toward your catch line. If it begins to look as though darkness will fall before you can get back, you might have to bivouac for the night. If so, start looking for an adequate place—with water and some sort of shelter, if possible—well before dark.

Being lost along with your party is bad enough, but it is even worse when an individual is alone and separated from the rest of the party. If you ever notice that someone is missing, the entire party should stop, stay together, shout, whistle, and listen for answering sounds.

WHAT IF YOU ARE LOST ALONE?

Again, the first rule is to *stop*. Look around for other members of the party, shout, and listen for answering shouts. Sound your whistle if you have one. If the only answer is silence, sit down, calm down, and combat terror with reason. One of the greatest dangers of being lost is panic, which can lead to making unwise and nonsensical decisions. Once you have calmed down, start doing the right things:

1. *Look at your map* to determine your location and plan a route home.

2. *Mark your location* with branches, a cairn, or other objects (see "Mark the Route If Necessary," above), and then scout in all directions, each time returning to your marked position.

3. *Prepare for the night* by finding water and shelter.

4. *Try singing* so searchers can hear you.

If you are lost, study the shape of the terrain and try to associate it with your map.

The odds are that you will be reunited with your group by morning. After a night alone, you may decide to hike out to a catch-line feature—a ridge, stream, or highway—that you picked out before the trip. If the terrain is too difficult to travel alone, it might be better to concentrate on letting yourself be found. It is far easier for rescuers to find a lost person who stays in one place in the open, sounds a whistle, and shouts periodically, than one who thrashes on in hysterical hope, one step ahead of the rescue party.

The decision whether to forge ahead or to stay put is strongly influenced by whether or not anyone knows that you are missing and where to look for you. If you are traveling alone, or if your entire party is lost, and no one knows you are missing or where you had planned to go, you have no choice but to try to find your way back, even if this involves difficult travel. If, on the other hand, someone responsible expects you back at a certain time and knows where you were planning to go and what route you planned to take, then you have the option of staying put, making yourself visible, and concentrating on survival while waiting for a search party to find you.

DON'T COUNT ON CELL PHONES

Many travelers carry their cell phones into the wilderness for an added level of safety. However, these phones do not work everywhere. They must be able to transmit and receive signals to and from the nearest cellular tower, which might be out of range. Coverage in a remote area may also depend on your particular service provider. Therefore, you should never trust a cell phone to be a dependable way of being rescued if you are injured or lost. Consider cell phones to be unreliable luxuries.

PLBs and satellite communicators (previously described in chapter 5) can be very helpful if you become hopelessly lost or need to be rescued due to accident, injury, or illness.

Survival

Your chances for survival depend on how well equipped you are. Numerous stories of survival and tragedy start with statements such as "I was sure glad I had my . . ." or "Too bad they did not bring a . . ." Over the years these crucial items of gear have developed into a codified list known as the **Ten Essentials**. The point of the Ten Essentials, originated by the

Mountaineers, has always been to answer two basic questions: Can you prevent emergencies and respond positively should one occur (items 1–5)? And can you safely spend a night—or more—outside (items 6–10)? Use this list as a guide and tailor it to the needs of your outing.

1. **Navigation system**: At minimum, a topographic map of the area and a compass. Depending on the nature of the party and the trip, consider adding an altimeter, a GPS device, downloaded digital maps, and a satellite communication device or personal locator beacon to contact first responders; also consider a whistle and route-marking materials.

2. **Illumination system**: A flashlight or headlamp, plus spare batteries and a spare bulb

3. **Sun protection**: Sunglasses, sun-protective clothing, and broad-spectrum sunscreen rated at least SPF 30

4. **First-aid supplies**: Items to treat possible backcountry illnesses and injuries you may encounter, such as bandages; skin closures; gauze pads and dressings; a roller bandage or wrap; tape; antiseptic; blister prevention and treatment supplies; nitrile gloves; tweezers; a needle; nonprescription painkillers; anti-inflammatory, antidiarrheal, and antihistamine tablets; a topical antibiotic; and any important personal prescriptions, including an EpiPen if you are allergic to bee or hornet venom

5. **Tools and repair kit**: At a minimum, a good knife, as well as other tools (e.g., a multitool, strong tape, cordage) depending on what gear/equipment you need to maintain

6. **Fire system**: At least one butane lighter (or waterproof matches) and a firestarter, such as chemical heat tabs, cotton balls soaked in petroleum jelly, or a commercially prepared firestarter

7. **Emergency shelter**: A rain shell, as well as a single-use bivy sack, plastic tube tent, or jumbo plastic trash bag

8. **Nutrition**: In addition to snacks, enough extra food to survive for at least an additional day more than planned

9. **Hydration system**: Adequate water plus the skill and equipment to find and purify additional water

10. **Insulation**: Enough extra clothing to survive the most severe night that you can expect in the area you will be visiting

Always consider the possibility that one member of your party might become separated from the rest of the group and will depend totally on his or her own equipment and skill for survival. It is therefore essential that all members of the party carry adequate food and equipment. It is equally important that all members of the party have the knowledge and skill to use all the necessary equipment (including the map and compass), rather than always relying on the skills of another. If someone gets lost, having the proper equipment and skills may make the difference between tragedy and a graceful recovery from the experience.

It is important to be prepared for unforeseen emergencies, such as getting injured or lost, and to have all the equipment and training necessary to survive such an experience. But it is even better to learn the tools of navigation, particularly the map and compass, to avoid getting into such a situation in the first place.

CHAPTER SUMMARY

In this chapter you learned about trip planning and keeping track of your position on your map to ensure that you do not get lost. Additionally, you learned the importance of telling someone responsible where you are going and keeping the party together. Finally, you learned about the gear and a few techniques for getting yourself back on track if you or your party ever does get lost.

SKILLS CHECK

See the appendix for answers.

1. **A linear feature that can guide you to your objective or back to your starting point is called a:**

   a. baseline   b. catch line   c. handrail   d. latitude line

2. **A feature that you can aim for on your return, which is always in the same direction as your desired direction of travel, is called a:**

   a. handrail   b. longitude line   c. catch-line   d. latitude line

3. **Route marking, such as by building rock cairns or tying surveyors tape to branches, should be:**

   a. done seldom, if at all   c. left in place if found
   b. removed on your return   d. all of these

4. **A planned deviation from your intended route, providing a faster and/or easier return route in the event of emergency, illness, or other unexpected event, is called a(n):**

   a. secondary route   c. primary route
   b. escape route   d. desperation route

5. **Telling a responsible person where you are going, what route you are taking, when you expect to return, and other trip details is:**

   a. rarely necessary   b. always necessary   c. never helpful   d. a waste of time

6. **Establishing and sticking to an agreed-upon turnaround time is:**

   a. required on guided trips   c. always a good thing to do
   b. never done   d. only for climbers

7. **Maintaining awareness of your location and where you are headed is called:**

   a. nosiness   c. excessive compulsiveness
   b. obtrusiveness   d. situational awareness

8. **On any wilderness adventure, you should always:**

   a. assign a "sweep" to watch for stragglers   c. keep the party together
   b. follow an agreed-upon route plan and turnaround time   d. all of these

9. **If you even begin to think that you might be lost, the first thing you should do is:**

   a. shout "help!"   c. continue on your present course
   b. stop   d. hope for the best

10. **The Ten Essentials is for:**

    a. climbers and hikers only   c. hunters and anglers
    b. only for climbers   d. all wilderness travelers

CHECK YOUR ANSWERS. How did you do? If you got all the questions right, then proceed with confidence to the next chapter! If you got some wrong or could not answer some, reread the pertinent sections of this chapter before proceeding on to the next.

CHAPTER 7

MORE ABOUT MAPS, COMPASSES & GEOMAGNETISM

CHAPTER OBJECTIVES

- Explain the latitude/longitude coordinate system.
- Describe the UTM coordinate system and explain how to use it.
- Describe the range, township, and section method of land survey.
- Show how to measure distance on maps.
- Explain how to use pace on wilderness excursions.
- Describe how to measure the grade of slope on maps and in the field.
- Explain how to get accurate, up-to-date declination information.
- Describe how and why declination is changing.
- Explain compass dip and how to cope with it.
- Demonstrate how to use clinometers.
- Describe features of some types of compasses not covered in chapter 2.

Latitude/Longitude Position System

The traditional latitude/longitude (lat/lon) system is used on both USGS topographic maps and marine charts. Another coordinate system, called Universal Transverse Mercator (UTM), is also used on topographic maps. Therefore, whereas the land traveler has a choice of defining position using either the lat/lon system or the UTM system, the nautical traveler using marine charts must use the lat/lon system. Lines of constant latitude are sometimes referred to as **parallels** (such as the 49th parallel, which defines the northern border of the United States from the state of

Washington to Minnesota). Lines of constant longitude running north–south are referred to as **meridians**.

The lat/lon coordinate system is based on angular positions on the surface of the Earth and has been used for centuries by mariners, cartographers, and land travelers. It is based on the accepted convention that there are 360 degrees (°) in a circle, so there are 360° around the Earth whether going in a north–south or east–west direction. Latitude is measured from 0 degrees at the equator to 90 degrees at the poles (90° N at the north pole, and 90° S at the south pole). Longitude is measured from 0° at the Prime Meridian (also called the Greenwich Meridian), which runs through the Greenwich observatory near London, United Kingdom, 180° both east and west until they meet in the Pacific Ocean.

Each degree is divided into 60 units called minutes ('), and each minute is divided into 60 units called seconds ("). A latitude of 74 degrees, 15 minutes, and 49 seconds north can be written N 74°15'49". This is the degrees, minutes, and seconds format, abbreviated H ddd.mm.ss: H for hemisphere (E, W, N, or S), ddd for degrees, mm for minutes, and ss for seconds.

One minute of latitude is equal to one nautical mile (6076 feet, 2025 yards, or 1852 meters). Since there are 60 seconds in a minute, 1 second of latitude is equivalent to about 101 feet (34 yards, or 31 meters). These numbers are often helpful in identifying your position on a topographic map or a marine chart. Modern usage has led to two other formats:

- **Degrees, minutes, and decimal minutes**: These are represented by H ddd.mm.mmmm. In the above example, divide the 49" by 60 to get 0.8167 minutes, and add it to the 15' to get N 74°15.8167'. This is the most convenient format for determining position on marine charts.
- **Degrees and decimal degrees**: These are represented by ddd.ddddH. Divide the 15.8167' in the above example by 60 to get 0.2636° and add it to the 74° to get 74.2636°N. This format is used on many GPS devices and is preferred by search-and-rescue groups.

Some applications, such as mapping apps and phone GPS displays, do not use the *N, S, E,* and *W* to indicate hemisphere, but instead use positive values for north latitude and east longitude, and negative values for south latitude and west longitude. (In chapter 5, the GPS screenshots in figures 5-1 and 5-2 show latitude and longitude in the degrees and decimal degrees format, with positive values for north latitude and negative values for west longitude.)

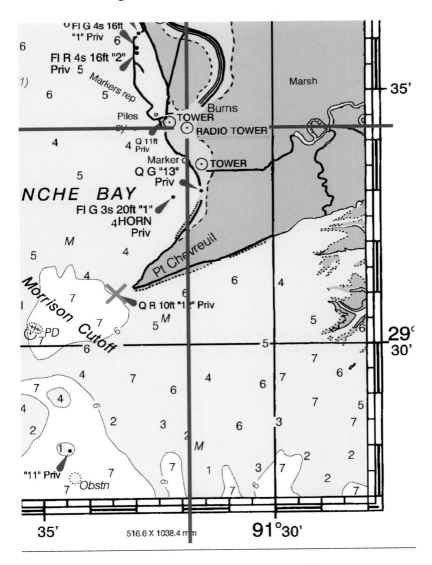

Fig. 7-1. *Marine chart for demonstrating latitude and longitude coordinates*

Figure 7-1 shows a portion of a typical US marine chart. The coordinates in degrees and minutes are identified by scales at the edges of the chart. In this example, marks are given for every half minute. Locations between these marks can be estimated visually. For example, the coordinates of "Radio Tower" can be found by drawing vertical and horizontal lines through that point to the chart edges, as shown. Its coordinates are visually estimated to be N 29°34.25' and W 91°31.8'. To convert to degrees and decimal degrees, divide the 34.25 and 31.8 minutes by 60 to get decimal degrees: 29.5708°N and 91.5300°W.

To convert degrees, minutes, and decimal minutes to degrees, minutes, and seconds, multiply the decimal portion of minutes by 60. In this example, the coordinates would then be N 29°34'15" and W 91°31'48".

Most older USGS topographic maps show the latitude and longitude using the degrees, minutes, and seconds format at all four corners of the map, and at two intermediate places along the top, bottom, and both sides. The N and W designations are not printed, since these are for the United States, where the latitude is always north and the longitude is always west. Some of the more recent USGS Topo maps show coordinates at the corners in the degrees and decimal degrees format.

Using the UTM Coordinate System

The UTM system is a grid of north–south and east–west lines at intervals of 1000 meters (3281 feet or 0.6214 mile), as shown in figure 7-2, which shows the lower-left corner of a typical USGS topographical map. Measurements in the north–south direction are called **northings**, and measurements east and west are called **eastings**. This is far more precise for USGS topographic maps than the lat/long system, because USGS maps only identify latitude and longitude coordinates every 2.5 minutes (approximately 2 to 3 miles or 3 to 5 kilometers). Without using a scale or ruler, you can usually "eyeball" your position to within about 100 meters (about 300 feet) using the UTM system, which is often close enough to at least get to within sight of your objective.

A northing is the number of meters north or south of the equator. An easting is the number of meters east of a certain reference line. This line is based on the **zone** number, which is shown in the lower-left corner of the map, as in figure 7-2.

For example, suppose you are climbing toward Glacier Peak in Washington State, and clouds obscure all visibility. You reach a summit but are not sure whether it is the true summit of Glacier Peak. You turn on your GPS device and let it acquire a position. The UTM numbers on the screen of your GPS device are as follows:

10 640612E   5329491N

The first number is the easting. The "10" is the UTM zone number. The numbers "640612E" indicate your position within zone 10. In figure 7-3,

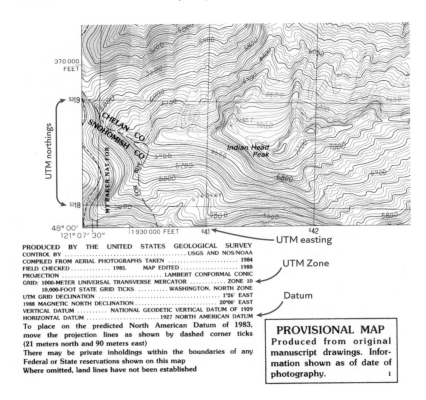

Fig. 7-2. *Lower-left corner of a USGS topographic map showing UTM zone and datum—partial eastings and northings are also shown.*

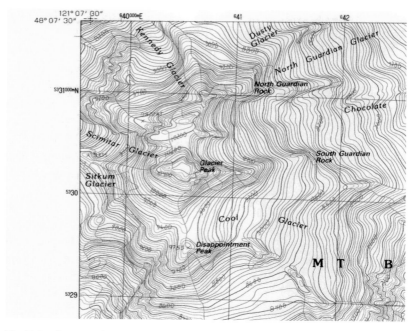

Fig. 7-3. *Close-up of a USGS topographic map showing the Glacier Peak summit area*

you can find the number "640000mE" along the top edge of the map. This is the **full easting** (except for the zone number). To the right of this is the number "641." This is a **partial easting**, with the "000" meters omitted. You can see that the number "10 640612E" on the screen of the GPS device is approximately six-tenths of the way between 640000 and 641000. Your east–west position is therefore about six-tenths of the way between the 640000 and the 641000 lines. Your position is somewhere on a vertical line running roughly through both Glacier Peak and Disappointment Peak.

Along the left edge of the map shown in figure 7-3 is the number "5331000mN." This is the **full northing**, which indicates that this point is 5,331,000 meters north of the equator. Below this is a line labeled "5330," and another labeled "5329." These are **partial northings**, with the "000" meters omitted. The second set of numbers displayed on the GPS device is 5329491N. This is a horizontal line about halfway between 5329 and 5330. The point where the easting and the northing lines

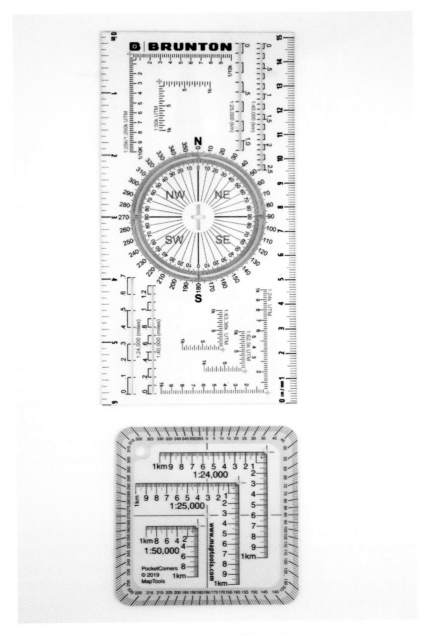

Fig. 7-4. *An example of map tools to measure UTM position*

Fig. 7-5. *An example of a compass with Romer scales*

intersect is your **point position**. Finding this point in figure 7-3 shows that you are on Disappointment Peak.

If you have difficulty "eyeballing" distances between UTM coordinate lines, there are special rulers and other measuring devices that can provide greater precision. You can purchase plastic scales to read UTM coordinates on 1:24,000 and other scale maps (see fig. 7-4), though this requires carrying one more piece of special equipment. Some compasses are equipped with scales to locate your position on maps; some of these have "GPS" in their model numbers. Other compasses have **Romer** scales for use with either 1:24,000 or 1:25,000, or 1:50,000-scale maps. The compass shown in figure 7-5, for example, has Romer scales for 1:25,000-scale and 1:50,000-scale maps, as used on many metric maps. Compasses with Romer scales of 1:24,000 are also available, though the difference between these two scales is so small that you can use a 1:25,000-scale Romer while using a 1:24,000-scale map, with only a very slight error.

Navigation Using GPS and UTM Coordinates

Suppose that you can identify your desired destination on the map but cannot actually see it in the field. You can then read the UTM position of the destination off the map and enter it into your GPS device as a waypoint. You can then get the GPS device to tell you the distance and direction to that place.

Going back to the Glacier Peak example shown in figure 7-3, suppose you wish to find the route from wherever you are to the summit of Glacier

Peak. From the map, you can see that the summit of Glacier Peak is about halfway between the eastings of 640000 and 641000, so you could estimate the easting as 10 640500 (the zone number is still 10). You can also see that the summit is about three-tenths of the way between the northings of 5330000 and 5331000, so you can estimate the full northing to be 5330300N. You can now enter the UTM coordinates of 10 640500E and 5330300N into your GPS device, and it will tell you the distance and direction to Glacier Peak.

Zone and Latitude Bands

The UTM **zone** is usually printed on USGS maps (see fig. 7-2, for zone 10). There are sixty zones, and each is 6 degrees wide. Zone 1 is for the area from 180° W longitude to 174° W, and its zone meridian (centerline) is 177° W. Zone 2 is from 174° W to 168° W longitude, with a zone meridian of 171° W, and so on. The centerline of each zone is numbered 500000mE. The reference for UTM eastings is a meridian located 500,000 meters west of the zone meridian.

Table 7-1. UTM LATITUDE BANDS AND RANGES

UTM band	Latitude range	UTM band	Latitude range
C	72–80 S	N	0–8 N
D	64–72 S	P	8–16 N
E	56–64 S	Q	16–24 N
F	48–56 S	R	24–32 N
G	40–48 S	S	32–40 N
H	32–40 S	T	40–48 N
J	24–32 S	U	48–56 N
K	16–24 S	V	56–64 N
L	8–16 S	W	64–72 N
M	0–8 S	X	72–84 N

Some GPS devices use a **latitude band** letter with the UTM system to indicate position relative to the equator. This system divides Earth into 8-degree-wide latitude bands from 80° S latitude to 84° N latitude (the northernmost band being a bit wider than the others). The bands are lettered from south to north, according to table 7-1.

> **Tip:** If you ever need to convert from one of these systems to another, there are several coordinate-conversion websites available. Two such sites are earthpoint.us and ngs.noaa.gov.

If the latitude band is used, the letter for that band is placed immediately after the zone number, such as 10T 0546379. Some GPS devices require using such a latitude band. Others merely ask you to indicate which hemisphere you are in, north or south. Due to distortion of the UTM grid lines near the poles, the UTM system is not defined north of N 84° or south of S 80° latitude.

Other Coordinate Systems

The area covered by the UTM system includes most of the world except Antarctica and Arctic regions north of Alaska's north coast. In those areas you can use the lat/long grid or the **Universal Polar Stereographic (UPS)** grid instead. This grid is very similar to the UTM grid, in that it expresses locations with a grid of 1-kilometer squares, and eastings and northings expressed in meters, just as with the UTM system. Some GPS devices have a single setting for both, such as "UTM/UPS" or "UTM UPS." The zone number is always zero for the UPS grid. The latitude band letters are A and B for the Antarctic region, and Y and Z for the Arctic region. Most GPS devices automatically switch from UTM to UPS when traveling north of N 84° or south of S 80°.

Since nautical charts and USGS topographic maps only use lat/long and the UTM or UPS systems, those systems are all that you need to know for wilderness travel. Two other coordinate systems are sometimes given as options of GPS devices: MGRS and MGRS Polar.

The **Military Grid Reference System (MGRS)** is used by the US military. It is essentially the same as the UTM system, except that some of the leading UTM numbers are replaced by letters. The last five digits of the MGRS easting and northing are the same as for the UTM system. For example, if your UTM location is 10T 0471523E and 5307108N, your MRGS location is expressed as 10T DJ 71523 and 07108. Note that the "71523" and the "07108" are the same in each system.

MGRS Polar is similar to the UPS grid, based on a grid of 1-kilometer squares for the polar areas outside the area of coverage for MGRS.

Range, Township, and Section

The primary surveying system used in most parts of the United States is the **range, township, and section system**. In this system, most of the United States is divided into regions called townships. This system is used in all the states west of the Mississippi River (except for Texas), as well

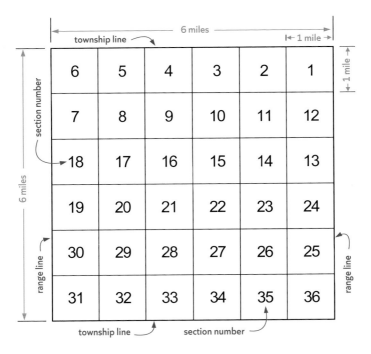

Fig. 7-6. *A township consists of a square 6 miles on each side that contains 36 sections. Each side of a section is 1 mile.*

as in Minnesota, Wisconsin, Michigan, Ohio, Indiana, Illinois, Mississippi, Alabama, and Florida.

A **township** is a 36-square-mile area. The township is divided into 36 one-square-mile **sections**. The sections are numbered from 1 to 36 in a zigzag pattern starting at the northeast corner of the township (see fig. 7-6).

Each township is identified by its location with respect to a baseline and a meridian in a local coordinate system. One example is the Willamette Baseline and the Principal Willamette Meridian, whose intersection is located in the Willamette Stone State Heritage Site near Portland, Oregon (see fig. 7-7). This point is used as the basis of the range, township, and section system throughout the states of Washington and Oregon. The location of each township in these states is referred to by its distance from the intersection of the Principal Willamette Meridian (a north–south line) and the Willamette Baseline (an east–west line; see fig. 7-8). A township whose northern boundary is three townships (18 miles) north of the Willamette Baseline is identified as T3N. If this area's eastern boundary is 30 miles east of the Principal Willamette Meridian, the township is identified

Fig. 7-7. *Marker on the Willamette Stone near Portland, Oregon, the center of the range, township, and section system of land surveying in Oregon and Washington*

as R5E. If a specific location within this township is in section 23, it is identified as section 23, township 3N, range 5E.

In locations where the land has been surveyed using this method, the boundaries between sections, townships, and ranges are usually indicated by light red lines on USGS topographic maps. The township and range boundaries are shown by red letters and numbers, such as R5E or T6N, near the edges of the maps. The sections are numbered from 1 to 36 with red numbers in the centers of the sections. In figure 7-9, for example, the location indicated by A is in section 36, T15N, R6E. Big Creek

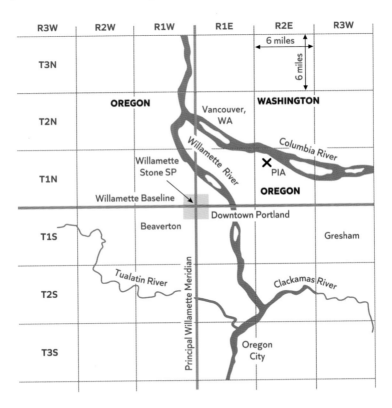

Fig. 7-8. *In the states of Washington and Oregon, township line boundaries are defined based on their distance north or south of the Willamette Baseline. Range line boundaries are defined based on their distance east or west of the Principal Willamette Meridian. These lines intersect just west of Portland in the Willamette Stone State Heritage Site, along Skyline Boulevard.*

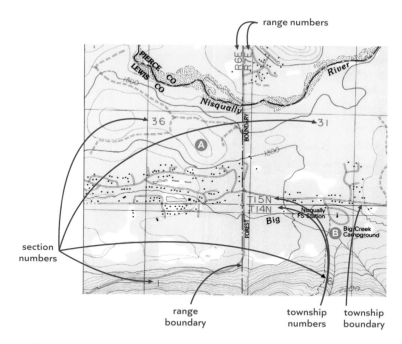

Fig. 7-9. *A portion of the USGS topographic map, showing section, range, and township numbers and boundaries*

Campground (indicated by B) is in section 6, T14N, R7E. Property surveys, timber sales, and some other forestry-related applications often use the section, township, and range system, though this system is not used on GPS devices.

Distance Measurement on a Map

You can easily measure distances on a map using the scales at the bottom of the map. To measure a **straight-line distance**, simply measure the length of the line joining the two points of interest using a scale of your compass or some other method, such as making two pencil marks on the edge of a piece of paper. Then compare this distance to one of the scales at the bottom of the map and read off the number of feet, meters, kilometers, or miles. *If the distance on the map is not a straight line, then you can instead use the lanyard attached to your compass,* or some other

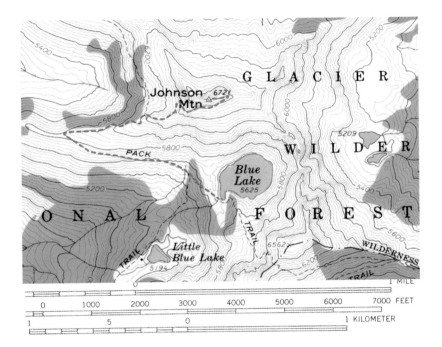

Fig. 7-10. *Measuring distance and finding elevation gain from a topographic map*

flexible material. Put the free end of the lanyard on one point on the map, then place the lanyard on the route to be measured, curving it along the trail, ridge, or other feature, until it reaches the other point on the map. Then straighten out the lanyard and place it alongside the desired scale at the bottom of the map.

While following trails with numerous short switchbacks, this method may be inaccurate, since the lanyard may not be able to keep up with all the tiny zigzags. In this case, your map measurement will at least give you a minimum distance, which may be enough information for your purposes.

Suppose you want to find the distance from Blue Lake to Johnson Mountain as shown in figure 7-10. You can measure the straight-line distance from the lake's outlet at its southwest tip to the summit of Johnson Mountain to find out how far a trip it would be. If you measure the distance of this route on the map and compare it to the scales at the bottom of the map, you should see that this corresponds to about 0.4 mile or

2200 feet (0.7 kilometer or 700 meters). (Try it yourself and see if you agree.)

Note that there is a trail from Blue Lake to the summit of Johnson Mountain. Though the distance to the peak will be longer via the trail, the travel will most certainly be easier. You can measure the map distance along the trail by placing the free end of the lanyard on the map at the outlet of Blue Lake, then curving the lanyard along the trail until it reaches the summit of Johnson Mountain. Then straighten out the lanyard and place it alongside whatever scale you want to use at the bottom of the map. The distance corresponds to about 1.3 miles or 7000 feet (2.1 kilometers or 2100 meters). Try it. Do you agree?

You can use either feet and miles or meters and kilometers for measuring or pacing distances. However, metric units are much easier to use, since you can mentally convert distances from kilometers to meters and vice versa by multiplying or dividing by 1000. Converting miles to feet or vice versa, on the other hand, requires multiplying or dividing by 5280 (the number of feet in a mile), which can be time-consuming and cumbersome in the field.

In the field, you can keep track of distance covered versus time to estimate your speed. Then you can use that knowledge to estimate how long it will take to complete the next leg of your trip. For example, suppose you have been walking for one hour and have traveled 3 miles. According to the map it is one more mile to your destination, so you should be there in about twenty minutes if you maintain the same speed.

Pace

It is occasionally necessary to go a certain distance in a given direction—for example, 300 feet (about 90 meters) in a northeasterly direction. Doing this requires a good estimate of your **pace**. All wilderness travelers should have a rough idea of the length of their pace. The length of your normal pace is the distance you cover when you walk two steps (one step with each foot) on level ground at a comfortable walking stride. To measure your normal pace, establish a starting point where you will be able to walk in a straight line on level terrain. Walk for ten full paces (ten steps with each foot), and mark the place where you stopped. Then measure the distance you walked. Divide that distance by 10 to get the length of your pace. For example, if the distance for ten full paces is 50 feet, then your pace is 5 feet. The normal pace for most adults ranges from 4 to 6 feet (about 1.5 to 2 meters).

Once you know your pace, you can use it to travel a given distance in the field. Suppose you want to travel 1000 feet, and you know your pace is 5 feet. Divide 1000 feet by 5 feet per pace, and the result is 200 paces.

> **Tip:** When using the length of pace in your travels, keep in mind that your actual pace can vary considerably due to differences in terrain. For example, your pace will be shorter when going uphill or through heavy brush, and longer when descending a good trail. So whenever you use your pace in navigation, be sure to make allowances for variations in the length of your pace with the terrain.

However, counting paces is a poor way to travel in the wilderness, since it is easy to lose count. If you concentrate hard enough to avoid losing count, you may miss important details of the route, such as key topographic features, and it may detract from your enjoyment of the trip. Keeping track of your location is far better achieved by closely observing the topography. If counting paces is necessary at all, we recommend that you use it only for short distances.

Slope (Grade) Measurement on a Map

By carefully measuring the horizontal distance between contour lines on a topographic map, you can estimate the steepness, or **grade**, of the slope as a percentage. You can find the grade of the slope by finding the vertical distance, or elevation gain, divided by the horizontal distance, and multiplying the result by 100. This is important for estimating the risk of avalanches (see "On Snow" in chapter 8) and for determining the feasibility of a particular route.

In the example shown in figure 7-10, we found the straight-line distance from Blue Lake to Johnson Mountain to be about 2200 feet. The elevation of Johnson Mountain is 6721 feet (as shown on the map), and the elevation of Blue Lake is 5625 feet. Subtracting 5625 from 6721 gives an elevation gain of 1096 feet. If you were to travel in a straight line from Blue Lake to Johnson Mountain, the grade of the slope would be the elevation gain (1096 feet) divided by the horizontal distance (2200 feet), multiplied by 100. This gives a grade of about 50 percent, which is a very steep grade. Note also that this 50 percent is merely an **average grade**. The first 200 feet of gain will be rather gentle, but the next 400 feet will be steeper, as can be inferred from the closer contour lines. Above 6200 feet, the slope eases up somewhat. Since the average grade is 50 percent and some of the route has a lesser grade, it is apparent that the steepest grade along this route will be even more than 50 percent.

If you instead take the trail from Blue Lake to Johnson Mountain, the elevation gain is the same: 1096 feet. But the distance that you measured earlier using the lanyard of the compass was about 7000 feet. The

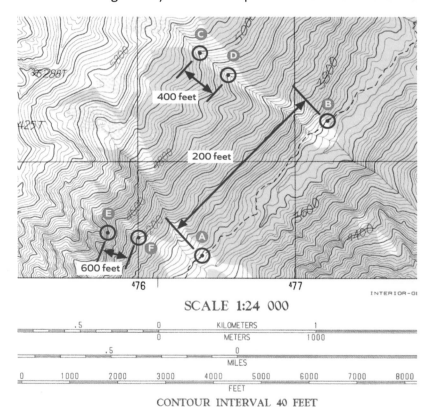

Fig. 7-11. *Measuring grade on a map*

average grade along the trail is therefore 1096 divided by 7000, multiplied by 100, or about 16 percent. This is a much more reasonable grade than that of the straight-line route.

These examples illustrate how to find the average grade over some distance. You can also find the **steepest grade** along any route using a similar procedure. Draw a line on the map indicating your proposed route. Pick out the place on this line that appears to be the steepest: the place where the contour lines are closest together. Identify two particular contour lines in this area—for example, two index contours (indicated by the heavier contour lines). The difference between these two lines is the vertical height of the slope. Now measure the horizontal distance between these same two lines. Compare this measurement to the feet scale at the bottom of the map. Then you can find the steepest grade of the slope by making the same calculation as above.

If you have a metric map, the contour interval will be in meters instead of feet. In this case, your horizontal distance must also be in meters. Use whatever units you want, as long as you use the same units for both the vertical and the horizontal measurements.

Figure 7-11 shows several examples of measuring the grade of the slope. Points A and B are at elevations of 3600 and 3400 feet, so the vertical elevation gain or loss is 200 feet. The horizontal distance on the map, which can be measured and compared to the scale for feet at the bottom of the map, gives a distance of 3800 feet. The grade is 200 feet divided by 3800 feet, multiplied by 100, which equals 5 percent. This is a gentle slope.

Points C and D are at elevations of 5000 feet and 4600 feet, so the vertical gain is 400 feet. The horizontal

Table 7-2. SLOPE GRADE AND ANGLE			
Grade	Angle	Grade	Angle
0%	0°	90%	42°
10%	6°	100%	45°
20%	11°	120%	50°
30%	17°	140%	54°
40%	22°	170%	60°
50%	27°	200%	63°
60%	31°	250%	68°
70%	35°	300%	72°
80%	39°	400%	76°

distance, when measured and compared to the scale for feet, gives 800 feet. The grade is 400 feet divided by 800 feet, multiplied by 100, which equals 50 percent, a steep slope. A grade of 50 percent corresponds to an angle of approximately 27 degrees.

Points E and F are at elevations of 4800 feet and 4200 feet, so the vertical gain is 600 feet. The horizontal distance is found to be 600 feet, which is the same as the vertical height of 600 feet. The grade is 100 per-cent: a 45-degree angle. This is a very steep slope. If the vertical gain is equal to the horizontal distance, the grade is 100 percent, and the angle of the slope is 45 degrees.

Measuring the grade of the slope is easy; it merely requires dividing the vertical gain by the horizontal distance (sometimes called "rise over run"). But expressing the result as an **angle**, in degrees, requires the use of trigo-nometry, which we would rather avoid in the field. For your information, the relationship between slope grade and slope angle is shown in table 7-2.

You can use this table (or trigonometry if you know it) for trip planning at home, but in the field you usually only need to know a few values. A 20 percent grade (about 11 degrees) is representative of a reasonably steep trail, such as one that gains about 1000 feet in 1 mile (5280 feet). A 50 percent grade has an angle of 27 degrees, and a 100 percent grade has an angle of 45 degrees. These three numbers can help you to determine the feasibility of negotiating a particular slope and can also help you to assess the risk of avalanche hazard (see chapter 8). A 50 percent grade is a very steep slope, well past the limit for hiking. Slopes steeper than 50 percent usually involve difficult scrambling or roped climbing. By the time the grade gets to 100 percent (45 degrees), you will probably need to belay for safety. On snow, you may need an ice axe even if the grade is less than 30 percent.

Wilderness travelers should know their limits regarding slope. Some-time when you are going up or down a slope that appears to be at your limit, and you feel uncomfortable about being there, mark that spot on your map. Once you get home, measure the grade of that slope for that location on the map. Then you will know your limit, and the next time you contemplate a route in unfamiliar territory, you will be able to measure its grade on the map to find out if it is within your comfort zone.

Where to Get Declination Information

As explained in chapter 1, declination is shown on most topographic maps. However, declination changes with time, and the declination for a location you are researching may have changed since a specific map was published.

The easiest way to get the correct present-day declination for any location is from the internet. The National Oceanic and Atmospheric Administration (NOAA) Magnetic Field Calculators website provides declination information for any place in the United States using only the postal ZIP code or the lat/long coordinates of the location. The latter can be found by looking at any corner of a USGS topographic map for the area of interest. You can also enter the names of many cities in the United States, Canada, Mexico, and other countries to find their latitude and longitude, and then their declination values. In addition to giving the magnetic declination in degrees, this website provides the present amount of annual change in declination. The website has occasionally changed names and locations in the past, so do a search for "NOAA magnetic declination" from your web browser. From the home page you can choose "Declination/Calculate."

DECLINATION OUTSIDE NORTH AMERICA

On the NOAA Magnetic Field Calculators website, the default latitude and longitude are north latitude and west longitude, which is appropriate for North America. It is possible, however, to enter southern latitudes and eastern longitudes, and therefore to find the declination for any point on the surface of the Earth. The website can also give you declination for any year from 2025 to 2030; this time span is updated every five years.

In most parts of the world, you can buy topographic maps with declination information. If you go to a foreign country where you cannot find the current declination, and if you do not have internet access, you can find a fairly close estimate of the declination from the world declination map shown in figure 7-12. The map is for 2025 and will be accurate to within two degrees for most locations outside of the polar regions until 2030. For an up-to-date version of the world declination map, visit the NOAA website, ncei.noaa.gov/maps/historical_declination.

Changes in Declination

Magnetic declination is caused by the motion of magnetic material (predominantly iron) in Earth's core. The soil and rock upon which we live is only a relatively thin crust. Beneath it is a solid **mantle** of rock extending to about 1800 miles (2900 kilometers) below the Earth's surface. Beneath this is a molten interior more than a thousand miles thick. In the center of our planet there is a solid inner core, rotating at a slightly different rate than the outer mantle. This rotation causes the molten material between the two solid portions to move. Since this material is magnetic, its constant motion creates a slowly varying magnetic field, with a magnetic north pole and a magnetic south pole, which are in different locations from the geographic poles located at 90 degrees north and south latitude. The motion of the molten material causes the locations of the magnetic poles to move as well.

The motion of the molten magnetic material is mostly random and unpredictable, so we cannot predict with certainty what the declination will be at any given place far in the future. However, Earth is very large, and changes take place slowly. Declination and its rate of change have been studied and recorded for many different locations over long periods of time to create the World Magnetic Model, which predicts future declination over a relatively short period of time, such as just a few years into the future. This is the basis for the NOAA declination prediction model at the website referred to above.

One example of how declination has changed over time is shown in figure 7-13, a graph showing the declination in Seattle, Washington, over the past two centuries, based on information from NOAA. You can obtain similar information for any other US location from the NOAA website. From the main "Magnetic Field Calculators" page, find and click on the "U.S. Historic Declination" tab. Then enter the range of dates and the location, and you should get a tabular listing of magnetic declination for the desired location for as long a time period as declination has been measured in the past.

It is very helpful for you to know how rapidly magnetic declination is changing for your area of interest. This knowledge will enable you to evaluate the accuracy of declination data printed on older maps and to determine how frequently you need to make adjustments or modifications to

Fig. 7-12. World declination map for the year 2025 . Red lines indicate east declination, and blue lines are for west declination. The green lines show the agonic line (zero declination).

your compass. You can obtain this information from the NOAA website, since it provides the declination rate of change as well as the declination once you provide the coordinates and desired date. If the rate of change is given in minutes per year, and you want to get the rate of change in degrees per year, divide the number of minutes by 60. For example, a rate of change of 7.2 minutes per year is 7.2 divided by 60, or 0.12 degree per year. The reciprocal of this value (1 divided by 0.12) is the number of years for a 1-degree change—in this case, 8.3. This means that in this example, the declination is forecast to change by 1-degree in the next 8.3 years.

If the *rate of change is in the same direction as your declination* (e.g., if declination is west and rate of change is west, as in Alabama), then the numerical value of declination is increasing. If the *rate of change and the declination are in opposite directions* (e.g., east declination and westerly rate of change, as in Wyoming), then the numerical value of declination will be decreasing.

For most of the contiguous United States and Hawaii, the predicted declination does not change more rapidly than about one degree every ten years at this time. This means that if you have an old map in these

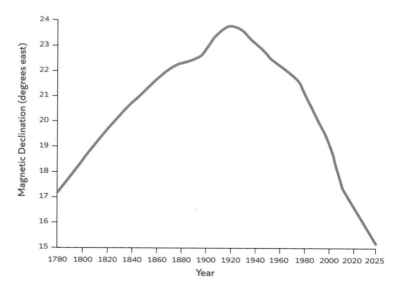

Fig. 7-13. *Historical declination of Seattle, Washington*

locations, you can most likely trust its printed declination if it is no more than about ten years old.

In Alaska, on the other hand, declination is changing much more rapidly. For example, in Prudhoe Bay, along the Arctic Ocean, the declination is predicted to change about one degree every two years; in Juneau, it is one degree every six years. Elsewhere in the state, it is between these values, such as about one degree in three years at Denali National Park and Preserve, and in four years in Anchorage.

Declination in Canada has an even wider variation in its rate of change: from about one degree every ten years in areas near the US border from British Columbia to Ontario, to one degree in one year in Resolute, in the Nunavut territory, and one degree every three to five years in Newfoundland, Labrador, and eastern Quebec. Travelers in these areas are advised to check their declination every few years.

South of the United States, the change varies from one degree in about ten years in northern Mexico, to one degree in seven years in Panama.

Dip

The magnetic needle of the compass is affected not only by the horizontal direction of Earth's magnetic field but also by its vertical pull. The closer you get to the magnetic north pole, the more the north-seeking end of the needle tends to point downward. At the magnetic equator, the needle will be level, while at the magnetic south pole, the north-seeking end of the needle tries to point upward. This phenomenon is referred to as **compass dip**. To compensate for this effect, most compass manufacturers purposely introduce a slight imbalance to the magnetic needles of their compasses, so that *their dip is negligible for the geographic area where they will be used*. Earth is divided into several **dip zones**, and compasses sold in each zone may be compensated for use in that zone.

If you buy a compass in one dip zone and try to use it in another, the compass may not work well because of the difference in dip. For example, if you buy a compass in North America or Europe and then try to use it in Chile or New Zealand, the difference in dip may be enough to introduce errors in your compass readings or even make the compass impossible to use.

TEST YOUR COMPASS FOR THE EFFECTS OF DIP

If you bring your compass to a faraway place, you should first try it out in an urban area as soon as you arrive there, to make sure it works properly before heading out into the wilderness. If it is adversely affected by dip, you may have to buy a new compass in the general area where you will be traveling before leaving town.

To avoid problems with dip, you can instead buy a compass ahead of time that is properly compensated for dip in the area you will be visiting. Some retail stores and online companies have, or can order, compasses compensated for whatever zone you will be visiting.

Some manufacturers produce compasses that are not affected by dip. These compasses have the term "global" in their names, or a notation on the package that the compass is corrected for dip anywhere in the world. If you intend to go on worldwide adventures, you might consider purchasing such a compass. Tables 2-1 and 2-2 identify some such compasses. Some compasses are made to overcome dip by replacing the metal needle with a plastic one and adding a magnetic hub.

Using a Clinometer

Some compasses are equipped with a **clinometer**, which measures angles of slope, or elevation angles, using a gravity-assisted needle. To use the clinometer on your compass, follow these steps:

1. Hold the compass with its long edge horizontal, and turn the bezel so that the numbered inside scale (usually the same scale used for declination adjustment) is at the lower long edge of the compass (see fig. 7-14).

2. Set either 90° or 270° at the index line, so that the needle points to zero when it is held level. (If the direction-of-travel arrow is pointing from left to right, as in fig. 7-14, then you will set 90° at the index line. If it is pointing from right to left, you will set 270° at the index line.)

3. Then, tilt the compass up or down. This will cause the clinometer needle to point to the number of degrees upward or downward.

There are several ways to use the clinometer. One way is to measure the elevation angle to a distant object. For example, suppose you are at the summit of a peak, and you see another peak of nearly the same elevation. You want to measure the angle from your position to that peak. Hold the compass with its long edge pointing toward the other peak, as you sight along the long edge of the baseplate (see fig. 7-15). Steady the compass on a rock or other stable object if possible. Tap the compass lightly to overcome any friction in the mechanism, and ask a companion to look at the clinometer needle from the side to read its elevation in degrees. In the close-up of figure 7-16, the angle is 34°.

> **Tip:** With a mirrored compass, you can read the angle to the object yourself by folding the mirror at a 45-degree angle, sighting along the edge of the baseplate toward the object, and reading the upward or downward angle in the mirror.

If you know the elevation angle to any point, such as another peak, then if you read the distance to that point off the map, you can use trigonometry to find the elevation (the number of feet or meters) that the object

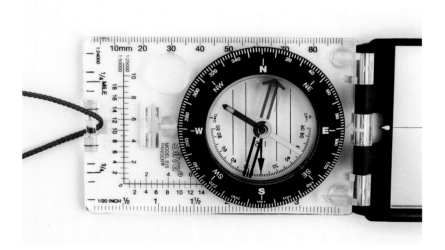

Fig. 7-14. *Clinometer bezel set for level conditions (reading 0°)*

is above you (elevation above yours equals the distance multiplied by the tangent of the elevation angle).

Another way to use a clinometer is to find the angle of a slope on which you are standing. Earlier in this chapter, you learned how to determine the angle of a slope from a map. The clinometer, however, can tell you the actual angle of the slope on which you are standing. As above, set 90° or 270° at the index line, so that it reads zero for the level condition. Then lay the long edge of the compass on the slope (fig. 7-17). Read the angle of the slope on the clinometer scale. Due to variations in the slope over small distances, it is best to place an ice axe, a branch, a trekking pole, or some other long object along the slope and then place the long edge of the compass along this object to get a better idea of the average slope.

Other Types of Compasses

Some baseplate compasses have rotating housings that are marked from 0° to 90° and back to 0°, and then to 90° and back to 0° again. These are called "quadrant" compasses, and some people prefer them.

Fig. 7-15. *Using a clinometer to find the angle of elevation of a distant object*

Fig. 7-16. *Close-up of a clinometer tilted upward—the measured angle is 34°.*

Fig. 7-17. *Using a clinometer to measure the angle of a given slope at a particular point*

Bearings taken with a quadrant compass are often expressed as the number of degrees east or west of north or south. For example, S 20° E, which means 20° east of south (or 180° minus 20°, equaling 160°). We do not recommend these for wilderness navigation, since most guidebook compass bearings are stated using the system of 0° to 360°.

For wilderness travel we recommend baseplate compasses. All of the examples of taking, following, measuring, and plotting bearings are based on the assumption that you are using such a compass. Most of the recommended compasses listed in chapter 2 are marked to 2-degree divisions, and it is unlikely that you can achieve better accuracy than that with those compasses. Many people have difficulty obtaining better than 5-degrees accuracy using compasses without a mirror. Even with a mirror, it is difficult to get accuracy consistently better than 2 degrees. If you need better accuracy for some particular activity, such as setting up a compass practice course, there are other, more precise compasses, most notably **optical sighting compasses**, which can provide better accuracy than baseplate compasses.

There are also battery-operated **digital compasses**. Some of these are more accurate and more precise than most baseplate compasses and are useful if the accuracy you need is not possible with a baseplate compass. Some wrist-worn altimeter watches also contain compasses, such as ABC (altimeter, barometer, compass) watches. They also tell the time. Some of these have adjustable declination, while others do not, so with some of these you may need to add or subtract declination (as described in chapter 2). Most of these are not baseplate compasses, so in order to use any of these with a map, you also need to have a protractor or a baseplate compass to measure and plot bearings.

Another type of wrist-worn compass device combines a GPS device with an ABC watch (see chapter 5). These are quite expensive, but they allow the user to determine precise position information (e.g., lat/long or UTM position coordinates) using the GPS feature and to measure and follow compass bearings using the digital compass, while monitoring altitude or barometric pressure with the altimeter/barometer sensor. Some of these have additional features, such as heart rate monitors and the ability to record training statistics.

We recommend that if you purchase such a wrist-worn compass, you also bring along a nonelectronic baseplate compass, as well as a paper map, on your wilderness adventures, so that you can use it to measure and plot bearings on the map and to avoid completely depending on an electronic device with limited battery power.

Lensatic compasses are used by the US Army and in rifle aiming. Lensatic compasses are specially optimized for military purposes and have dials marked in both mils and degrees. (There are 6400 mils in a 360-degree circle, or approximately 18 mils to a degree.)

Lensatic compasses do not have adjustable declination corrections, so the user must mentally add or subtract declination to convert between magnetic and true bearings. These compasses have markings only every 5 degrees and do not have transparent baseplates, so they cannot be used as protractors to measure and plot bearings on a map. For these reasons, we do not recommend lensatic compasses for wilderness navigation.

If you already have a lensatic compass and are proficient with it, you can use it to navigate in the wilderness. However, we encourage you to at least try out a baseplate compass. You may appreciate its advantages for wilderness navigation.

CHAPTER SUMMARY

This chapter covered material well beyond what is generally needed in casual trail hiking, including much more detail regarding maps, compasses, and geomagnetism. If you have read this chapter, you must be a serious student of backcountry navigation. We encourage you to read chapter 8 as well, to prepare for adventures off the well-maintained trail.

1. **What is the lat/lon position of point X in figure 7-1 at the start of this chapter?**

   a. in degrees, minutes, and decimal minutes (H ddd.mm.mmmm)
   b. in degrees and decimal degrees (ddd.ddddH)
   c. in degrees, minutes, and seconds (H ddd.mm.ss)

2. **What are the UTM coordinates of point A on the map shown in figure 7-18?**

3. **What are the UTM coordinates of point B on the map?**

4. **What topographic feature is shown at UTM coordinates 10 649400E, 5265600N?**

5. **What is the elevation of the point located at UTM coordinates 10 649400E, 5263200N?**

6. **What are the section, township, and range coordinates of point C?**

7. **What human-related feature is in section 32, township 24N, and range 15E?**

8. **What is the dominant topographic feature in section 8, T23N, R15E?**

9. **What is the straight-line distance between points D and E in: Miles? Feet? Kilometers?**

10. **What is the distance along the creek from point F to point G in: Miles? Feet? Kilometers?**

11. **What is the elevation change between points H and I in feet?**

12. **What is the straight-line distance from point H to point I in feet?**

13. **What is the grade, in a percentage, between points H and I?**

14. **What is the grade, in a percentage, between points J and K?**

15. **What is the average grade, in a percentage, between points L and M?**

16. **What is the grade of the steepest part of the route between points L and M?**

17. **Using only the world declination map in figure 7-12, what was the approximate declination in the very center of Spain on January 1, 2025?**

18. **Using the NCEI Magnetic Field Calculator website, what was the 2025 declination of Madrid, Spain? What is the rate of change of declination, in minutes per year, and in what direction?**

19. **If a declination is 15° E and its declination change is 0.25° E per year, how long will it take for the declination to change by 1°? At that time, what will be the new declination?**

20. **If a declination is 10° W and the declination change is 12' E per year, how long will it take for the declination to change by 1°? At that time, what will be the new declination?**

CHECK YOUR ANSWERS. How did you do? If you got all the questions right, then proceed with confidence to the next chapter! If you got some wrong or could not answer some, reread the pertinent sections of this chapter before proceeding on to the next.

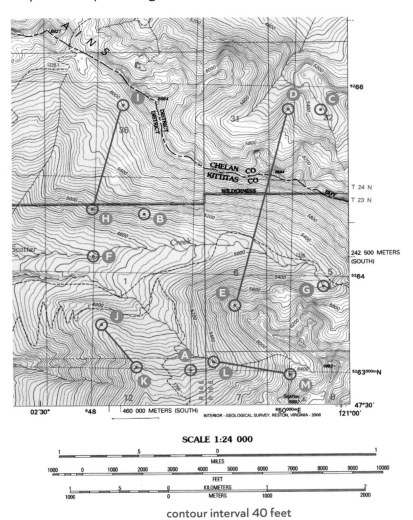

Fig. 7-18. *Map for chapter 7 Skills Check*

CHAPTER 8

WILDERNESS ROUTEFINDING

- Learn how to properly prepare for trips in the wilderness.
- Explain how to determine an appropriate turnaround time.
- Learn how to routefind on the trail, in the forest, in the desert, in alpine areas, and on snow and glaciers.
- Explain how to cope with extended periods of phone or GPS use with no means of recharging them.

Trip Planning and Preparation

Routefinding begins at home. Before heading out the door, you need to know not only the name of your wilderness destination but also a great deal about how to get there and back. This information is accessible to anyone who takes the time to seek it out—from guidebooks, maps, online sources, and people who have been there.

Any wilderness trip requires a **route plan**—that is, a well-thought-out procedure for how you will navigate to your destination and back. This includes handrails that you will be following, baselines or catch lines that you could head to in the event of an emergency, route-marking materials, compass bearings that you might need to follow, GPS coordinates of waypoints of crucial locations, downloaded maps and routes, and any other navigational aids.

Up-to-date guidebooks provide critical information such as a description of the route, the estimated time necessary to complete it, elevation gain, distance, and potential hazards. Travelers who have previously made the trip may be able to tell you about landmarks, hazards, and routefinding difficulties. Useful details are packed into maps of all sorts, including US Forest Service, road, aerial, sketch, and topographic maps. For a trip into an area that is particularly unfamiliar to you, more preparation is needed. This might include scouting into the area, making observations from distant vantage points, or studying aerial photographs or satellite imagery.

If the route comes from a guidebook or from a description provided by another person or a website, *plot it out* on the topographic map you will be carrying, noting trail junctions and other important points. It can help to highlight the route with a yellow felt-tip pen, which does not obliterate map features. Additional maps or route descriptions marked with notes about any more up-to-date information should be taken with you, along with the topographic map. In selecting the route, consider the season, weather and route conditions, the abilities of your party members, and the equipment available.

Do not let outdated information ruin your trip. *Check beforehand with the appropriate agencies about roads and trails*, especially closures, and also about off-trail routes, regulations, permits, and camping requirements.

One of the beauties of planning your adventure using maps and electronic devices is that you are tracing your route virtually. Once en route, you should have a pretty good idea of what hazards and obstacles lie ahead.

TURNAROUND TIME

Every wilderness adventure, however simple or sublime, must *have a predetermined, agreed-upon turnaround time*. This is the time of day when the party must turn around in order to return to the trailhead, camp, or other planned destination before dark. Everyone in your group should know this time and agree to it. Your objective plays an important role in the determination of this time. For example, if your destination is a car parked at a trailhead above the tree line, then you have an extra half hour to work with because it will still be light for about a half hour after sunset. However, if your destination is a campsite that you must set up in a thick forest, then you need to be more conservative. Visible light in a thick forest can dim about a half hour *before* sunset. Furthermore, you will need time to set up camp, purify water, prepare dinner, and plan the route for the next day.

Turnaround time should be based on the amount of available light during the day. In order to determine your safe turnaround time, first find the time of sunset. Then figure out how long you think it will take for you to get from your objective to the trailhead or camp. Add in an hour or two for lunch breaks and rest stops. For a level route, your time out and back will be nearly equal. On a steep climb, a good general rule is that it will take half the time to descend as it took to ascend the same route. Add the descent time to your anticipated ascent time and add in an hour or so for unplanned emergencies. For example, suppose you plan on a four-hour ascent time with two hours of descent time, on a day when the sun rises at 8 a.m. and sets at 6 p.m. If you start at 8 a.m. and allow an extra hour for good measure, this puts your turnaround time at 3 p.m. at the latest. With more experience you will learn the capabilities of your team members, but it is wise to start out conservatively for maximum safety.

On a typical glacier or snow climb, your turnaround time may be as early as 10 a.m. to avoid soft snow conditions on the descent. This often entails a predawn start. If the ascent is expected to require eight hours, with four hours of descent time, you may want to return to camp by noon, which would necessitate a midnight start time.

RETURN ROUTE

As a general rule, it is best to return from your objective using the same route that you take to your objective; you will be knowledgeable about route conditions, trail junctions, and any potential routefinding pitfalls in both directions. That said, however, there are times when you might not want to follow the same route back from your objective. For example, the route out might be a challenging technical climb, and it makes sense to follow an easier route back. Or perhaps you have chosen to take a scenic-loop trip on which you will never step on the same section of the route twice. Such trips can be incredibly interesting and satisfying but require extra caution.

If you do not follow the same route on your return, be sure to carefully study the entire route beforehand, and be aware of places where you might get off the correct route. Keep careful track of the amount of route remaining, given the pace at which you will be traveling. If there is any

Everyone in your group should agree on the turn-around time, when the party must turn around in order to return to your planned destination before dark.

doubt as to whether you will be able to complete the route in the allotted time, you may have to turn around before your halfway point, or potentially hike out in the dark over unfamiliar terrain (which is not recommended).

On the Trail

When following trails, be sure to *make a mental note of all trail junctions,* or jot down such essential information as you hike, as can be done on a small notebook preferably made of waterproof paper. Some junctions are indistinct, unmarked, or obscure. Others, though marked with signs, are easy to miss if you are in a hurry or not paying close attention. When following a good trail through nondescript territory, it is easy to get into mental autopilot, in which you just keep on walking without taking much note of the features you are passing. In such conditions, it is easy to miss trail junctions and wander off onto the wrong trail. Try to avoid this by remaining alert to your surroundings and always searching for trail junctions and other noteworthy features.

At clearings in the forest, trail junctions, stream crossings, passes, and other known locations, *locate your position on the map* (i.e., orient yourself). Be observant of the topography that you pass, and always have your topographic map available without having to remove your pack. For example, you may see a ridge or a gully coming down a mountainside, and you can glance at your map to note that you are passing such a feature.

When traveling in a group, follow reasonable precautions to prevent anyone from getting lost, such as keeping the party together or in close proximity, assigning a responsible person known as a "sweep" to travel behind the slowest member, instructing party members to wait at important points along the way, and other measures covered in more detail in chapter 6.

When the trail becomes lost in snow, blowdowns, overgrown brush, or rocks or shale, there are still ways to find it and stay on track. One way is to look for tree **blazes**—slashes, usually made by an axe (or sometimes by a paintbrush or spray paint), normally on trees about 6 feet (2 meters) or so above ground level, or on rocks on the ground. Another telltale sign is **prunings** that occasionally are visible, where tree limbs have been cut during trail maintenance operations. If neither of these helps you to stay on the trail, ask yourself, "If I were a trail, where would I be?" Trail build-ers usually locate trails on the *easiest terrain*, with a minimum of ups and downs, and requiring the least amount of effort. Remembering this may help you to relocate the trail. If you do lose the trail in brush, woods, or snow, then you should immediately stop, retrace your steps, and locate the last known trail position. It is often tempting to keep pressing on, with the notion that the trail will eventually emerge. But this is rarely the case. *Go back, find the trail, and then start the process of finding the true route to your destination*, whether back on the original trail or by some other route.

Even if the trail is muddy or full of puddles, we strongly recommend that you *stay on the trail*, walking right through the puddles, even if it means getting your feet wet. (The inconvenience of this practice is lessened by wearing appropriate footwear: good, solid, waterproof boots that will not soak through when you walk through water, or lightweight trail shoes that dry easily and quickly.) Walking off the trail to find dry spots eventually cre-ates multiple parallel paths and can create a severe human impact on the wilderness. In addition, be careful not to damage trailside vegetation—for example, take rest stops at places with rocks or logs, or at open, bare areas, rather than at places where you might damage trailside vegetation. Practice sound leave-no-trace principles to *minimize the impact of your presence*.

In the Forest

The moment you step off the road or trail and enter the forest, remind yourself that you are leaving your handrail, and you need to look for another one. The new handrail could be a topographic feature, such as a ridge, gully, or stream. In the total absence of a real, physical handrail, you can follow an invisible, abstract handrail such as a contour line (by keeping level, neither gaining nor losing elevation) or a compass bearing. If you do this, be sure to make a note of the elevation and/or bearing that you are following. Never merely wander off into the woods with no clear idea of the direction in which you are headed. You will also need a new baseline; this might be the road or trail that was your previous handrail.

It is best to try to *follow topographic features* when choosing a route in the forest. To avoid heavy brush, try to follow ridges and old growth

Stay on the trail whenever possible, even if it's muddy, to minimize the impact of your presence.

timber with open understories. Gullies, watercourses, and second growth may be choked with lush, difficult vegetation. You may encounter remnants of trails from time to time. If so, take advantage of them, since doing so may save you time and energy. But keep in mind that the destination of such trails may well be different from yours, particularly if you are following game trails. If the trail starts to deviate too much from your intended direction of travel, be prepared to leave it and head back to off-trail travel.

It may sound self-evident, but always remember that if you know where you are, you are not lost. So always *keep track of your position* using topography, time, vegetation, elevation, and any other means at your disposal. For example, you might jot down the following notes as you follow the route to your objective:

- Into woods at elev 2900 ft and bearing of 250°
- At elev 3500 ft travel level terrain at 310°
- Ascend forested ridge to broad bench at 4800 ft

Be sure to consult your map at frequent intervals to find each topographic feature that you encounter. Record your route in your notebook or on your map. Noting the direction of the slope may be of particular value in determining your position when known landmarks are obscured by forest or fog. The route will look entirely different on your return, but with the aid of your map, compass, notebook, and perhaps your altimeter or GPS device, you should be able to get back to your starting point without difficulty.

Mark the route if necessary. When traveling in the forest, it is particularly unlikely that you will follow exactly the same path on your return as on your way in, unless the topography of the area is very distinct. For this reason, it is essential to use natural materials such as branches, rocks, and logs, or biodegradable markers such as toilet paper, which deteriorates without leaving a trace (see chapter 6).

If you have a GPS device, take the time at the start of your trek to establish a waypoint or landmark. This may be possible at the road where you leave your car. If not, then at least read the UTM coordinates off the map and enter this location as a starting point. Later, if necessary, you can establish a new position and use the device to determine the distance and direction back to your starting point.

Remember to keep your map and compass handy as you travel in the forest. If you carry them in your pack, you will not use them as often as you should, since you will not want to stop frequently to remove your pack. If the route is difficult, with brush, fallen trees, or other obstacles to climb over and under, do not carry your compass with its lanyard around your neck, due to safety concerns (see chapter 2).

Enjoying the forest in the winter, early spring, or late fall can be a wonderful experience. The air is crisp and cold. Snow covers the forest floor. The bugs are gone, as are the majority of travelers. However, there is one distinct disadvantage to traveling through a forest with snow obscuring the trail: routefinding can be extremely challenging. With snow over the trail and landmarks and other objects obscured by forest, the route can be difficult to follow. Wands are very hard to follow in a forest. Further, GPS devices may not work well in a dense forest. Your map and an altimeter may be your best tools.

Begin honing your skills by traveling on snow-covered trails that you are familiar with. When en route, continually *ask yourself where you would be if you were a trail*. The moment that you are in unfamiliar terrain, retrace your route to a point that you are familiar with. If you know the direction to your destination, then blaze your own trail, but do not expect that your tracks will be recognizable for the return (see "The Bootprint" later in this chapter). You may need to find a new, and better, route for the return. Keep an eye out for trail markers, trail signage, blazes in trees, and significant landmarks on which to take compass bearings. Be on the lookout for signs of trailcraft, such as sawed logs, bridges, severed limbs, and other signs of human travel or construction. Slow your pace and be diligent. Take existing footprints with a grain of salt; they are just another clue as to where the route may go. Always assume that the travelers who made the existing footprints were lost, until you prove otherwise. Reorient yourself with the smallest sign of a trail—a bridge, a trail marker, or other landmark—and, most importantly, routefind with an open mind.

When hiking in the desert, don't assume you will always have good visibility for routefinding.

In the Desert

Routefinding in the desert can be easy when clear weather conditions allow you to see far-off landforms. But you should never count on such conditions. Sudden sandstorms and downpours occasionally occur, and if you assume that you will have good visibility for all of your routefinding, you can easily get into trouble. For this reason, it is crucial for you to *follow well-established trails or other handrails, or definite topographical features*, rather than to assume that you can always just aim for far-off visible features.

A prime consideration for any desert travel is the proximity to water. A good guideline is to carry at least one gallon (four liters) of water per person per day unless a dependable source of drinking water is available. However, there is a practical limit to how much weight you can carry, so the availability of good water along your chosen route is often a deciding factor in desert routefinding, particularly for extended trips.

The wide-open views in the desert make GPS usage easy and dependable. Under these conditions, it is most advisable to carry and frequently *use a GPS device* of some kind. However, GPS devices do not work well, if at all, in deep canyons. If following a poorly marked trail or dubious natural features, it might be advisable to leave your GPS device on continuously so as to record your exact track. If you plan on doing this, be sure to carry an extra supply of batteries, preferably longer-lasting lithium cells. You can also carry a supply of previously charged nickel–metal hydride (NiMH) rechargeable cells—a wise investment if you use a lot of battery-operated devices. Just remember to recharge them before leaving home.

In Alpine Areas

Many of the same suggestions offered above for forests and deserts also apply to alpine areas. First, find and *follow a route using natural topographic features* wherever possible. You can use ridges, gullies, streams, and other readily identifiable features as handrails. Even if the route appears obvious, pause now and then to look at the map and find your location, and observe the topographic features that you are using on your route. The sudden arrival of clouds may turn an obvious route into a challenging navigational problem. Mark your route on the map in pencil, perhaps even noting the time of arrival at various places along the route. Remember that you should be able to identify your position on your map as accurately as possible at any point of your trip.

If you must deviate from natural topographic features, then use your compass to *find the bearing* that you will be following on the next leg of your trip. Make a note of this bearing in your notebook or on the map. If you have an altimeter, look at it often and follow your progress on the map. Ask yourself frequently what you would do if fog or clouds suddenly came in and obscured your view of the return route. How would you recognize key points at which you need to make crucial route changes? Should you be marking the route at such places? Should you be saving GPS waypoints?

In selecting the route, try to *minimize the impact of your party on the terrain*. Many alpine areas are particularly fragile. Some delicate woody plants, such as heather, grow only a fraction of an inch (a few millimeters) each season, and a few thoughtless footprints may wipe out an entire season's growth. If there is any trail at all, use it to minimize your impact. In the absence of a trail, try to stick to rocks, scree, talus, or snow to avoid stomping on fragile vegetation. If you must travel over alpine growth, disperse your party to minimize your personal impact as much as possible.

Open alpine areas are excellent places to use GPS devices. At every rest stop, and at important route changes, take the opportunity to turn on your device and obtain a satellite fix. Save these locations as waypoints. In the event that you wander off route, you may be able to acquire a new position fix. Then your device will be able to tell you the new bearing to any of your previously established waypoints.

On Snow

Always be aware of potential avalanche conditions. If a slope has snow on it, then it has the possibility of sliding, often with deadly results. Slopes with a grade of about 50 percent to 170 percent (an angle of about 25° to 60°) have a high likelihood of sliding, so always *be aware of the grade of the slope*—and not just the slope you are on, but more importantly the slope above you. The most extreme hazard occurs when the slope grade is about 70 percent to 100 percent—an angle of 35° to 45°—so be particularly wary on slopes in this range. (Chapter 7 includes techniques for measuring the grade of a slope on a map, as well as using a compass's clinometer to measure the actual angle of a slope.) Slopes of 60 degrees (about 170 percent) or greater present very little risk, since new snow regularly sluffs off them.

Many times, you can *follow previous bootprints* in the snow to find the proper route. Even if they are several days old, an observant navigator can sometimes distinguish them from sun cups and still follow the route. Vague bootprints will sometimes have a uniform indentation and may have a distinct, subtle ring of dust in them. But it is still your responsibility to know your approximate location and direction at all times. It is entirely possible that the bootprints you follow were made by a person headed to a different destination from yours. A wilderness navigator who uses the excuse "It's not my fault that we're lost—I was following tracks!" needs to read this book again before venturing out on another trek.

Following a route that has been put in on a snowfield is often academic: simply follow the bootprints. But prints are rarely permanent and can degrade quickly under some conditions. Wind and newly fallen snow can obliterate tracks, sometimes only a few seconds after they are created. The sun, especially at higher altitudes, can also erase tracks. This can be particularly surprising on a summer day when you thought that your descent following your own tracks would be a piece of cake, only to find on your return trip that your footprints have melted out and become intermingled with existing sun cups. Fortunately for the wilderness traveler, with a little homework and a few navigational tools, you will be able to find your way back.

The best tools for routefinding on snow are your map and compass. By taking bearings on an intermediate objective such as a pass or rock outcropping, you can navigate toward that objective even if clouds move in. If you write down those compass bearings, then on the return trip you can easily follow the back bearings for each consecutive leg and make it back. Another tool for routefinding on snow is the altimeter. The clouds have rolled in, and you press on until reaching what you hope is the summit. But a quick check of the altimeter shows that you are 700 feet (200 meters) lower than the printed summit on the map (assuming a stable barometric pressure). A look at the map shows a false summit 500 feet (150 meters) lower than the true summit. It is likely that you have not quite made it yet.

A GPS device can be a big help on snow and in whiteouts. It can give you a fairly good idea of where you are and where to go, but only if you have saved the proper waypoints. By entering important positions, such as the location of your camp, the device can guide you to your objective and back. On long trips when conserving battery power is a concern, you can obtain the proper bearing to your destination from the GPS device, set the bearing on your compass, turn the device off, and then follow the bearing using your compass.

Capable, cautious wilderness navigators will develop the skills to use their map and compass, altimeter, GPS device, and possibly other devices (e.g., wands, whistles) as a complete system, rather than as independent tools.

WANDS

You may occasionally have difficulty retracing your ascent route when on an indistinct snowfield where your bootprints are obliterated by wind, sun, or new snow. In this case, a dependable way to follow your ascent route is to follow tall, thin stakes called wands. *Think of a set of wands as a portable handrail that you place on the ascent.* Most people make their own wands out of 3-foot green bamboo sticks purchased at any gardening store. Two bags of darkly stained bamboo sticks will usually yield twenty-five really good wands, once you have weeded out the flimsy and knotted ones. (Any potential wand deemed inappropriate for alpine use will happily serve its life in your garden.)

To make the wands more visible, cut a 6-inch piece of brightly colored duct tape and make a flag at the top of the stick by folding the duct tape back over itself (fig. 8-1). To discern your wands from anyone else's, you can mark each flag with your initials and the date (e.g., "MB 2025"). Wands can be carried behind the compression straps of your pack, where you can reach them for easy placement without removing your pack.

Wands are placed with the descent in mind, so *place wands where they will be visible on the return trip.* It is always better to place the wand on the top of a small rise rather than in a hollow. Beware of background features such as rocks or trees that can cause the wand to blend in with its surroundings. Your

Fig. 8-1. *A wand with a duct-tape flag*

wands should be as easy as possible to spot and follow. One helpful trick is to *angle the wand slightly toward the previously placed wand.* On your return, if you cannot see the next wand, you will have a pretty good idea of the direction to it. If you still cannot see the next wand, then have the party wait at the last wand and cautiously search for the next one, always remaining in sight or within shouting distance of the rest of the party. Wait until you find the wand, and then proceed to the next one. It is all too easy for a party to rush down an indistinct snow slope and lose their wands under poor conditions. Once lost, it can be difficult to find the wanded trail again.

If the party is roped up, then a good general rule is to place the wands no farther apart than the combined length of the rope teams. If the terrain does not warrant roping up, then the safety margin must be increased and the wands placed so that you can see at least one, and preferably a second, wand from each successive wand. It is easiest to find successive wands if they are placed at approximately equal intervals, so that you know where and when to look for them. This might require counting paces between wands to space them at predictable intervals.

If you find that you are running out of wands, then try to supplement the wands you have by using natural terrain features. Perhaps you can place a few wands at regular intervals on an indistinct snowfield until you reach a distinct ridgeline. Then you can follow the ridgeline without placing any wands until you come to its end. At this point you may elect to build a small temporary cairn to mark the route. Another way to conserve wands is to set one wand in a good spot, then take a compass bearing toward your previous wand and place a second wand about a foot (30 centimeters) from the last one, with the wands lined up to point toward the previous one. To follow the course back, simply take the compass bearing that the two wands create and follow that bearing to the previous wand(s). In this way you can place pairs of wands farther apart than single wands.

Your party should always carry enough wands to make it to your destination. The number of wands depends greatly on the length and complexity of the route. It is not uncommon for a party to carry a hundred wands for a long route. If you are in a party of four, that is only twenty-five wands per person.

Wands left behind are considered litter. Always be sure to *remove all your wands on the descent.* Conversely, *never remove someone else's wands,* since they are depending on them for their descent. If you encounter some-one else's wand that has melted out of the snow and has fallen over, place it upright again. Do not expect to follow somebody else's wands. They may remove them on the descent ahead of you. Your party should be responsi-ble for getting to and from its destination using only its own resources.

It is possible that you may run out of wands before you reach your des-tination. Perhaps the conditions warrant more wands than you had antici-pated. If this is the case, your party must decide a proper course of action. Perhaps you can use another form of navigation, such as taking a bearing from the last placed wand toward your known destination. Careful study of the map or an altimeter reading may help. Perhaps a GPS device can show you the way, though it is not a panacea; it may not be accurate enough to indicate the position of your last placed wand, and in cold conditions its display may go blank, so do not depend solely on it.

On Glaciers

As the route ascends high above the tree line and onto snowfields, route-finding becomes easier. Snow covers the talus and protects the fragile meadows. But a new hazard may be lurking underneath: **crevasses**. Many times, there is a traditional roping up point that divides the nontechnical ascent from the technical. At other times, in the absence of a terminal or lateral moraine, and especially in early season, it may be difficult to deter-mine exactly where the snowfield ends and the glacier begins. Find your position on the map, and check your elevation as indicated on your altim-eter or GPS device. Does your map show that you are on a glacier? (Note that some glaciers have boundaries that may have changed since the map was last updated, so do not trust the marked boundary if you are using an old map.) *Rope up for all glacier travel!* The next section assumes that you are tied in to the climbing rope.

The tools and techniques used for routefinding on snow can be used on glaciers as well. You will have two primary concerns while traveling on gla-ciers. One is that *the route should be as efficient as possible*—as straight a line as the team can handle—leading to your objective. The second, and sometimes contradictory, one is that *the route should avoid objec-tive hazards*—such as areas below major icefalls, cornices, melt streams, bergschrunds, and avalanche slopes—and should travel over as few cre-vasses as possible.

Many times, just as on snow, *you can follow a previous route*. Often, on popular glacier routes, the route will be a well-paved "trail" along the glacier's surface. Sometimes it is so good that it forms a veritable pathway, making an otherwise steep and tricky traverse an easy walk.

Occasionally, if the route is old or if it is late in the season, the route will end at a gaping crevasse, the sign of a collapsed snowbridge. A new route will have to be made over or around the crevasse in order for you to con-tinue. Always be prepared to put in the route yourself.

Crevasses tend to be most plentiful around turns and obstructions and near the sides of the glacier. Often, the center of the glacier may have a more homogeneous bedrock base and thus fewer, albeit deeper, cre-vasses. Crevasses tend to form in groups with their attitude perpendicular to the direction of glacier flow.

Sometimes, if there is a crevasse that has just begun to show itself, a previous party may have placed two wands together forming an X. This is a warning to steer clear—a crevasse is probably looming underneath the snow surface. The proper way to travel around a known crevasse is to steer wide around it, a route called an **end run**. Oftentimes on a glacier, a cre-vasse will exist beneath an otherwise unexplained dip in the snow surface. As you approach, keep the climbing rope taut and probe the snow deeply with your ice axe, and look through the hole to see if there is a crevasse. Step wide over the dip. Tread lightly and step over anything that you sus-pect may be a crevasse. Remember too that if you are putting in the route, then it is likely that many more will follow your path, perhaps even in your very footsteps. You should craft a route that is manageable for all wilder-ness travelers, not just for the long-legged or athletic.

While ascending, *keep the descent path in mind*. If you jump over a cre-vasse with uneven sidewalls, be sure that all party members will be able to jump over it again on the descent. Additionally, you want your route to last for several days, not hours, and summertime glacier surface melt is often significant, up to several inches per day. For this reason it is best to make long end-runs and cross on thick snowbridges.

For glacier travel, choose a route that is as efficient as possible while avoiding objective hazards.

Most prudent summit attempts on glacier routes are begun a few hours before the coolest part of the day. With a cold air temperature, snowbridges are firmer and the glacier surface is more likely to be frozen over, making for smooth cramponing instead of slushy postholing. Time your start so that your descent is completed well before the heat of the day. It is common for summit teams to leave high camp between midnight and 4 a.m., summit, and return to high camp before noon.

With a large party on an unblazed glacier route, it may be advantageous to send a scouting party ahead to put in the route. Alternatively, a small side trip might yield an excellent vantage point from which to view the glacier from a distance. At such a point you may more easily see the big picture of where the route should be heading as well as any major obstacles, such as icefalls, that must be avoided.

Moats and Bergschrunds

The area between moving snow or ice masses and stationary features like rock ridges, moraines, and summit ice caps is often defined by the presence of a moat or bergschrund.

Moats form when rock, radiated by the sun, warms and melts the snow near it. Moats can be dozens of feet deep and can be difficult to see from below. Moats have a propensity to swallow up ankles, legs, unsecured equipment, and sometimes climbers. If you are on a snow surface approaching a rock feature, always assume that a moat is lurking. As you approach the rock, probe the snow with your ice axe and look through the hole to see if the rock is visible. Step wide over the gap. It may be advantageous to cross the precipice laterally or even downhill to get a wider stride.

Bergschrunds commonly occur high on a mountain face. They are formed when the moving ice or snow mass separates from the summit ice or rock. Early in the season they may be filled in with snow and crossing them may be simple; you may not even notice them. But later in the season they can present challenging routefinding problems. Sometimes a snowbridge may cross a bergschrund. Other times the safest course is to steer wide around them, perhaps even climbing on the smooth rock at its end. Deep and wide bergschrunds can present such a significant routefinding obstacle that the team may have to turn back—there is not always a way around them.

Long Treks: Thru Hikes, Long Loop Trips, and Section Hikes

During the last century, before GPS, many people hiked the Pacific Crest Trail, the Appalachian Trail, and other long thru and section hikes, as well as long loop trips such as the Wonderland Trail around Mount Rainier, all without GPS. How did they do it? They carefully studied maps for these trips; read route descriptions containing tips, cautions, and special instructions; and then carefully planned out every leg of the hike, considering the time of year, snow conditions, access points, and myriad other details. You will likely take your well-charged phone with at least one GPS app on your hike, but when preparing for such an outing, you should carefully consider what you would do if your phone ran out of power, fell off a cliff, suffered electronic failure, got wet, or became otherwise inaccessible. There are strategies available to deal with this:

- As mentioned in chapter 5, battery life can be greatly extended by using GPS only infrequently, when needed, and keeping it turned off the rest of the time. This is especially important for long trips, when you may need to go many days, weeks, or even months without recharging your phone.
- Carry a spare battery pack or two to recharge your phone if its battery becomes exhausted. An additional option is to carry a solar charger to soak up solar energy during daytime hiking to recharge your spare battery pack, which can then be used to recharge your phone when at camp for the night.
- Carry an inexpensive and lightweight dedicated GPS device. Leave it turned off unless your phone battery dies or is otherwise nonfunctional or lost. Then use it to display your UTM position, and find your position on your paper topographic map, as described in chapter 7. Carry extra batteries (usually 2 AA cells). Note that lithium batteries are lighter and last longer, though they are somewhat more expensive.
- Instead of a dedicated GPS device (or in addition to it), wear a solar-powered GPS watch, which can charge its battery anytime the sun is shining.
- Satellite messengers or communicators (described in chapter 5) determine your position by GPS and can send messages to others if you

require rescue. You can also use these devices to determine your UTM position and then find it on your topographic map without using the rescue capability.

The Bootprint

Every bootprint tells a story. *Bootprints can tell you a lot about who and when someone has walked the path before you.* As you travel, pay attention to who is in front of you and what type of prints they are leaving. Pay attention to the size, direction, and depth of the print; the shape of the sole; the distance between prints; and the style of the tread pattern. Was the person who left those prints tall or short? Was the person wearing a big, heavy pack, causing deep prints? Or was the person wearing tennis shoes? Do you know what your own bootprint looks like? Could you follow it back after other people have made new prints on top of it?

How can you tell if your party is the first of the day on any particular route? Well, if the only prints that you see are facing you and look like they may have been made the previous day, then chances are that you are the only ones up there.

How far ahead is the next person? In the forest, if the tracks that you are following are filling in with water from a puddle, then the hiker is right around the corner. If the prints have fir or pine needles or leaves on them, then they are older. If the tracks in the mud are drying and becoming less defined, then the party must be at least a few hours ahead of you.

How does the energy level of your teammates measure up? If someone is ahead of you and wearing crampons, then you can make very specific observations about their gait. Are there two long parallel streaks leading to the rear crampon marks? This may indicate a party member who is getting tired. The important point here is to be aware. Use all the information that is available, not just what is obvious.

Once, a large group was ascending a trail. One member had to stop to make a clothing adjustment. He told everyone to continue on. One other experienced party member waited with him. The two began to follow after a few minutes. The route began to be obscured by snow, but the tracks from the party ahead were fresh and easy to follow. Then the tracks split into two different directions. Both sets of tracks were made at about the same time. (It was a popular route.) "Which way do we go?" the less experienced man asked. The more experienced man knelt down and carefully examined the two paths, without disturbing them. He reached down and touched some of the prints, testing them and seeing how the snow had formed in the spaces between where the cleats of the boot had left the prints. "They went this way," the experienced man pointed. "How do you know?" the other man asked.

The more experienced man explained that he had noticed that the last person in the group that they were following was a woman who was wearing the same style of boot that he was wearing, only it was about five sizes smaller. The odds of someone else having the same size and style of boot as that woman at that hour on that trail were low. Therefore, they went that way. All they needed to do was to follow those same prints. The two followed the unique prints and after a few minutes they caught up with their group. If the two of them had simply blundered along, unaware of the tracks that they were following, they might have missed their group's turn and might have had to double back after not finding them. But because of experience and awareness, they were able to find their group with little trouble.

Know your own bootprint. And know the bootprints of other members of your party. You may not be able to pick out every step taken along the way, but chances are you will be able to discern between ascending and descending prints, and more importantly, any changes in the prints that you are following.

CHAPTER SUMMARY

Orientation and navigation are sciences that can be easily mastered by anyone who takes the time and makes the effort to learn map reading and the use of a compass and other navigational tools. Practice and time spent on these subjects will enable anyone to become proficient with them. Routefinding is different. It is an art.

Some individuals seem to be born with an innate gift for finding and following a route on trails, through the forest, in the desert, in alpine regions, and on snow and glaciers. The natural abilities of such people can be greatly enhanced if they thoroughly learn the sciences of orientation and navigation, through mastery of the map, compass, and other tools. Such knowledge can enable a good routefinder to become a great one.

Some people are not blessed with a great natural ability in routefinding. But there is hope for them too. Through study and practice, they can also become proficient in orientation and navigation. They can even become experts in the use of the map, compass, altimeter, and GPS if they spend the time and effort required to do so. Then, with time and experience, they can acquire much of the art of routefinding, particularly if they travel in the company of good routefinders, observing and learning as they do. Above all, there is no substitute for experience and practice.

We encourage you to reread and study this book carefully, learning the sciences of map reading, compass use, orientation and navigation, the altimeter, and the GPS. But this book is not enough. Practice and considerable experience are necessary to thoroughly develop the skills and acquire the self-confidence that comes with repeated use of the principles described in this book. So go out into the wilderness and put the principles of *Wilderness Navigation* into practice—at first, perhaps, on good trails, then progressing to off-trail travel with ever-increasing routefinding challenges. Eventually, whether you are a natural-born routefinder or not, you can become thoroughly adept at map and compass use and will at least possess the knowledge and experience to avoid getting lost—and to recover gracefully from the experience if you ever do. And who knows, someday you might become a great routefinder, able to successfully navigate your way to any destination, solve all problems along the way, and make it back to your starting point with little difficulty or incident—because you planned it that way.

SKILLS CHECK

See the appendix for answers.

1. A wise turnaround time should be based on:

a. the time of sunset
b. the estimated time to get to the objective and return
c. added time for rest stops and emergencies
d. all of these

2. If you realize you have lost a trail, how can you find it?

a. Look for blazes on trees.
b. Look for prunings.
c. Ask yourself, "Where would I be if I were a trail?"
d. all of these

3. **A snow slope with a grade of 70% to 100% has what likelihood of avalanche?**

    a. minimal
    b. high likelihood

    c. worst avalanche hazard
    d. none of these

4. **A slope with a grade of 170% or greater has what likelihood of avalanche?**

    a. worst hazard
    b. impossible to predict

    c. high likelihood
    d. minimal

5. **A slope grade of 70% to 100% has an angle of:**

    a. 25° to 60°   b. 35° to 45°   c. 100° to 170°   d. 70° to 100°

6. **A slope with an angle of 45° has what slope grade?**

    a. 25%   b. 45%   c. 50%   d. 100%

7. **What can be used on snow and glaciers as a portable handrail?**

    a. climbing rope
    b. rock cairns

    c. wands
    d. footsteps in the snow

8. **When planning a route in the desert, what factor is more important than when you are in other terrain?**

    a. a mostly level route
    b. avoiding gullies

    c. good views
    d. proximity to water

9. **When traversing alpine areas, which factor becomes more important than when you are in other terrain?**

    a. minimal impact
    b. proximity to water

    c. mostly level route
    d. cold temperatures

10. **When you encounter puddles in a trail, you should:**

    a. step off the trail onto trailside vegetation
    b. walk through the puddles

    c. place branches or rocks to step on to keep your feet dry
    d. remove your shoes or boots and walk barefoot through the puddles

CHECK YOUR ANSWERS. How did you do? If you got all the questions right, then proceed with confidence with your wilderness navigation skills! If you got some wrong or could not answer some, reread the pertinent sections of this chapter before heading out into the wilderness.

Appendix: Answers to Skills Checks

CHAPTER 1

1. A: c   B: b   C: d
    D: c   E: a   F: b
    G: a   H: b   I: a

2. J: 3600 feet   K: 2300 feet
    L: 2560 feet   M: 2160 feet
    N: 2460 feet   P: 3400 feet
    Q: 4520 feet   R: 4280 feet

3. c

4. b

5. c

CHAPTER 2

1. b

2. c

3. b

4. d

5. a. 45°   b. 225°
   c. 135°   d. 315°

6. a. 13° W   b. 4° W   c. 11° E
   d. 10° E   e. 18° E   f. 8° E

7. 74°

8. 208°

9. Lundin Peak

10. Cave Ridge

CHAPTER 3

1. Chair Peak, 6238 feet

2. 192°

3. B

4. H

5. 250° to 270°

6. Upper Melakwa Lake

7. 2°

8. d

9. 165°

10. About 1800 feet. No, the topography would be difficult, due to steep travel. Instead, follow the ridge to the north, to Hemlock Pass, and intersect the trail there.

CHAPTER 4

1. convenience (on your wrist at a glance), multiple functions in single piece of equipment, greater precision (resolution)

2. no battery, functions even in extreme low temperatures, generally less expensive

3. c

4. a

5. b

6. Set it to a known altitude.

7. c

8. d

9. b

10. It compensates for temperature changes at a constant altitude, but not if you are changing altitude.

CHAPTER 5

1. d

2. any three of the following: inexpensive since most already have phone, access to downloadable maps, rechargeable batteries, large screen

3. more rugged, less temperature dependent, user-replaceable batteries

4. instant, convenient access; no need to wait to acquire satellites; longer battery life

5. b

6. d

7. decrease timer-off time, decrease screen brightness, use sparingly, disable unused apps or functions

8. cell phone (if in range of antenna), PLB, satellite messenger, satellite phone

9. less expensive to purchase, some have no subscription costs

10. any three of the following: some are full GPS devices, can send messages to friends and family, additional message options, two-way texting

CHAPTER 6

1. c
2. c
3. d
4. b
5. b
6. c
7. d
8. d
9. b
10. d

CHAPTER 7

1. a. N 29°31.1', W 91°33.3'
   b. 29.5183°N, 91.5550°W
   c. N 29°31'6", W 91°33'18"
2. 649000mE, 5263000mN
3. 648400mE, 5264600mN
4. cirque, stream origin
5. 5600 feet
6. section 32, T24N, R15E
7. County Line
8. two summits and saddle between them
9. 1.3 miles, 7000 feet, 2.1 kilometers
10. 1.8 miles, 9800 feet, 2.9 kilometers
11. 1000 feet
12. 4200 feet
13. 24%
14. 20%
15. 40%
16. 67%
17. 0° W
18. 0°30' E (0.5°); 10° E per year
19. 4 years; 16° E
20. 5 years; 9° W

CHAPTER 8

1. d
2. d
3. c
4. d
5. b
6. d
7. c
8. d
9. a
10. b

Acknowledgments

We wish to express our appreciation to everyone at Mountaineers Books who helped create this book. Emily White has been phenomenal. Her attention to detail, flexibility, and out-of-the-box thinking has helped us bring our vision to life. We would like to thank the entire staff of Mountaineers Books, with whom we have worked for more than forty years, on both *Freedom of the Hills* and *Wilderness Navigation*. Thanks to project editor Beth Jusino, copyeditor Sarah Breeding, and proofreader Erin Moore, who all made us sound smart and intelligible. Kate Basart has created a beautiful book layout. Jennifer Shontz's illustrations, and Chloe Dorgan's updates, bring the work to life. Photographer Silas Crews captured color images that had only existed in our minds. Ellis Failor-Rich and Bart Wright stepped up to make detailed, updated declination maps. And lastly, to the unsung heroes of the Mountaineers Books warehouse who pick our books, as well as hundreds of other titles, to ship to the world.

We also want to thank the fantastic staff at Feathered Friends for their input, especially Tessa McGee for the thoughtful suggestions that have been included herein.

Bibliography

The books listed here are only a few of the many books available on wilderness travel. These particular books are mentioned because they provide additional insight into the general subject of wilderness travel, including safety, first aid, marine and mountain weather, avalanche safety and rescue, and other areas of interest to those who enjoy the wilderness experience.

Avalanche Essentials: A Step-by-Step System for Safety and Survival, by Bruce Tremper, Mountaineers Books, 2013.

The Avalanche Handbook, 4th edition, by David McClung, Mountaineers Books, 2023.

Avalanche Pocket Guide: A Field Reference, by Bruce Tremper, Mountaineers Books, 2014.

Crevasse Rescue Pocket Guide: A Field Reference, by Mountaineers Books, 2016.

Emergency Essentials Pocket Guide: A Field Reference for Survival, by Mountaineers Books, 2016.

Hiking Safety Handbook, by Art Hogling, Colorado Mountain Club, 2023.

Marine Weather Pocket Guide: A Field Reference, by Jeff Renner, Mountaineers Books, 2017.

Mountain Weather Pocket Guide: A Field Reference, by Jeff Renner, Mountaineers Books, 2017.

Mountaineering: The Freedom of the Hills, 10th edition, by Mountaineers Books, 2024.

Mountaineering First Aid: A Guide to Accident Response and First Aid Care, 5th edition, by Jan Carline, Steve MacDonald, and Martha Lentz, Mountaineers Books, 2004.

Staying Alive in Avalanche Terrain, 3rd edition, by Bruce Tremper, Mountaineers Books, 2018.

Photo Credits

Primary photographer **Silas Crews**: pages 46, 47, 48, 49, 53, 54, 60, 62, 81, 98, 121, 151, 152, 171, 172, 173

Authors **Bob Burns** and **Mike Burns**: pages 21, 22, 23, 24, 134, 156, 173, 193

The following photographers from Unsplash also graciously provided photos for this book. They retain the copyrights to their images: **Sergei A**: page 204; **Dhilip Antony**: page 40; **Maël Balland**: pages 105, 126; **Zoshua Colah**: page 91 ; **Kalen Emsley**: page 144; **Tim Foster**: page 182; **Antonio Gross**: page 37; **Ali Elliott**: page 12; **Collin Lloyd**: page 210; **Alex Moliski**: pages 8, 96, 188; **Egor Myznik**: page 108; **Greg Rosenke**: page 185; **Wilifried Santer**: page 178; **Alessio Soggetti**: page 197; **Annie Spratt**: page 138; **Dennis Yu**: page 74

The following figures were adapted from ***Mountaineering: The Freedom of the Hills,*** published by Mountaineers Books: Figures 2–1, 2–6, 2–7, 2–14, 2–16, 2–19, 2–20, 3–2, 3–3, 3–7, 3–8, 3–9, 3–10

Index

About the Authors

A fifty-year member of The Mountaineers, **Bob Burns** has hiked, scrambled, climbed, and snowshoed extensively in the western states and provinces of the United States and Canada. He has been teaching classes on the use of map and compass since the 1970s. He is a previous author or coauthor of six revisions of the navigation chapter in *Mountaineering: The Freedom of the Hills.*

Mike Burns is a rock, ice, and expedition climber; filmmaker; drone pilot; and outdoor gear consultant who has climbed throughout the Pacific Northwest, Colorado, Alaska, Canada, Mexico, Argentina, Nepal, Pakistan, Iceland, and India, including a first ascent in the Himalaya and numerous long section hikes and mountain circumnavigations. For the past thirty years, he has been an instructor and lecturer on the technical aspects of climbing, section hiking, and navigation. He has written numerous articles for *Mountaineer* and *Climbing* magazines. He is also a previous contributor to *Mountaineering: The Freedom of the Hills.*

MOUNTAINEERS BOOKS including its two imprints, Skipstone and Braided River, is a leading publisher of quality outdoor recreation, sustainability, and conservation titles. As a 501(c)(3) nonprofit, we are committed to supporting the environmental and educational goals of our organization by providing expert information on human-powered adventure, sustainable practices at home and on the trail, and preservation of wilderness.

Our publications are made possible through the generosity of donors and through sales of 700 titles on outdoor recreation, sustainable lifestyle, and conservation. To donate, purchase books, or learn more, visit us online:

MOUNTAINEERS BOOKS
1001 SW Klickitat Way, Suite 201 • Seattle, WA 98134
800–553-4453 • mbooks@mountaineersbooks.org • mountaineersbooks.org

An independent nonprofit publisher since 1960

 Mountaineers Books is proud to support the Leave No Trace Center for Outdoor Ethics, whose mission is to use the power of science, education, and stewardship to ensure a sustainable future for the outdoors and the planet. The Leave No Trace program is focused specifically on human-powered (nonmotorized) recreation. For more information, visit www.lnt.org.

OTHER TITLES YOU MIGHT ENJOY FROM MOUNTAINEERS BOOKS

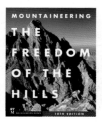

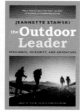